THE
GIRL'S OWN
BOOK

published in cooperation with

Old Sturbridge Village

APPLEWOOD BOOKS

The Girl's Own Book was first published in 1834.

ISBN: 978-1-55709-134-5

Thank you for purchasing an Applewood Book.
Applewood reprints America's lively classics—books
from the past that are still of interest to modern readers.
For a free copy of our current catalog, write to:
Applewood Books, Box 27, Carlisle, MA 01741.

20 19 18 17 16 15 14 13 12

Library of Congress Cataloging-in-Publication Data
Child, Lydia Maria Francis, 1802-1880.
   The girl's own book/ by L. Maria Child.
        p.   cm.
   Orginally published: Carter, Hendee and Babcock, 1834.
   ISBN: 978-1-55709-134-5
   1. Games for girls.   2. Amusements.   I. Title.
   GV1204.998.C48   1992
790.1'94-dc20   92-10815
                                          CIP

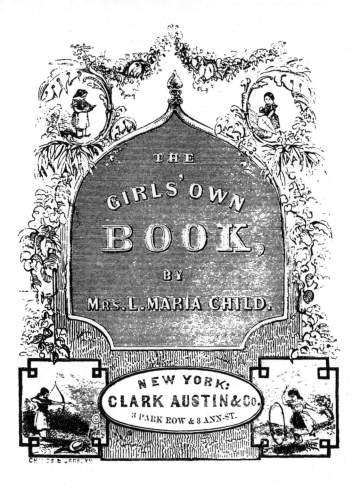

THE GIRLS' OWN BOOK,

BY

MRS. L. MARIA CHILD.

NEW YORK:
CLARK AUSTIN & Co.
3 PARK ROW & 3 ANN-ST.

PREFACE.

———

This little book has been compiled with an earnest desire to make it useful, in all respects, to its readers; but I have relied on my own judgment and experience: therefore there is little doubt of numerous imperfections.

Perhaps I have erred, in trying to please all; and may thus, like the old man in the fable, succeed in pleasing none. Some will say there is too large a proportion of games; others will smile at the directions for sewing and knitting; some may complain that the frequent recommendation of active exercises will tend to make their children rude and disorderly; others will think too much is said about gracefulness and elegance; some will call the conundrums old, others will say they are silly, and others, that they should have been entirely excluded. I knew I could not avoid numerous criticisms, and, therefore, I did not write with the fear of them before my eyes.

In this land of precarious fortunes, every girl should know how to be *useful;* amid the universal dissemination of knowledge, *every mind should seek to improve itself to the utmost;* and in this land of equality, as much time should be devoted to *elegant accomplishments*, *refined taste*, and *gracefulness of manner*, as can possibly be spared from holier and more important duties. In this country it is peculiarly necessary that daughters should be so educated as to enable them to fulfil the duties of a humble station, or to dignify and adorn the highest. This is the reason why I have mingled a little of every thing in the Girl's Own Book.

If the volume proves attractive, a large proportion of the credit must be ascribed to the generosity of the publishers, and the skill and good taste of the artists who have been employed. The drawings of the automata were prepared by D. C. Johnson. The illustrations of the Games were drawn by Mr. Graeter: to those who have been his pupils, nothing need be said in praise of his spirited and graceful sketching.

Whether *my* share in the formation of this little book is deserving of popular favor, I am extremely doubtful; I am only sure that it contains nothing to corrupt or mislead.

P. S.   To all my readers, little ones especially, a merry Christmas and a happy New-Year.   MRS. CHILD

CONTENTS.

CONTENTS.

HOT CROSS BUNS.

Hot cross buns! hot cross buns! one a penny two a penny! hot cross buns! hot cross buns!

hot cross buns ! one a penny, two a penny, hot cross buns.

LITTLE NANCY.

Little Nancy said to me one day, come and

play upon your Guitar.

Little Nancy said to me one day come and

play upon your Guitar.

Which goes tang tang tang, which goes tang tang tang, which goes

tang tang tang which goes tang; which goes tang tang tang which goes

tang tang tang, which goes tang tang tang ta ma.

LITTLE GIRL'S OWN BOOK.

GAMES.

THE BUTTERFLY AND THE FLOWERS.

THIS beautiful little play is a great favourite in France. All
those who are to join in it take the name of some flower or
insect; and they then choose one to begin the game, who is
called the Butterfly. This game may be played either by
young ladies and gentlemen, by little girls and boys, or by little

girls alone. If there are gentlemen or boys, they always take the part of insects; ladies and little girls take the names of different flowers; if little girls play it by themselves, it is necessary, in order to avoid confusion, to have the insects ranged on one side, and the flowers on the other, in the form of half circles each. The one who is chosen to represent the Butterfly should be in the centre of the circle. There are eight rules in the game, which must be carefully observed.

1st. The insects shall be represented by boys, if any boys take part in the play; and the flowers shall be represented by girls.

2d. No flower or insect must be mentioned, unless there is some one in the company who is called by the name of that flower or insect. Thus, if there are six little girls who play the game, and it is agreed that one shall be called Lily, another Balsamine, another Violet, another Pink, another Daisy, and another Snow-drop, it will not do for any of the players to mention a rose in any way; if they do, they must pay a forfeit, because there is no one who represents a Rose. The six on the other side may be called Caterpillar, Wasp, Dragon-fly, Bee, Lady-bug, and Beetle; whoever should happen to mention a Mosquito, in this case must pay a forfeit.

3d. The name of no flower or insect must be mentioned twice.

4th. At the mention of the *gardener*, all the little girls representing flowers must stretch out their right hands, to show

how the flowers open their leaves and rejoice at the refreshing water which the gardener-brings. All those who bear the name of insects, on the contrary, must jump up and step back a little, to show that they are afraid of him.

5th. At the word *water-pot*, all the flowers must rise and lift up their heads, as if eager for the water; and all the insects must drop on one knee and hold their heads down, as if afraid of being drowned.

6th. All the players must observe this: at the mention of the *sun*, every one must rise, as if to hail his presence, equally delightful to flowers and insects.

7th. Each one must speak the moment he hears his name.

8th. After taking the positions prescribed in rules 4, 5, and 6, every one must remain as they are until some insect or flower is again mentioned. (See the example of the Wasp.) When any of these rules are broken, the company demand what forfeit they please.

There are no rules concerning what shall be said by the different actors: that must depend upon the wit and skill of the players. The beauty of the game is very much increased by each insect and flower saying something appropriate to its own character, either original, or quoted from books.

I will give a few sentences by way of example, and leave it to the good taste and intelligence of my little readers to provide themselves with such a variety as the occasion may require.

After all is arranged according to the above rules, the But-

terfly begins by saying, " Oh ! beautiful flower, so pure and
sweet ! what shall I say in praise of thee ? They tell me I am
capricious, that I am always roaming from flower to flower;
but indeed, I could repose many minutes on the leaves of the
white *Lily*."

Here the Lily, hearing her name, interrupts him :

" Your flattery is a sign that you are an inconstant coxcomb.
Faithful friends say but little about their love. Of what value
are your silly compliments to a flower who opens her petals
only to the pure rays of the SUN ? (*Here all the players rise.*)
Your flattery displeases me almost as much as the stinging
sarcasms of the *Wasp*."

Here the Wasp, who with the others have kept standing
until a *name* was mentioned, re-seats himself, and speaks :

"Whatever flowers may say, they are never so well pleased
as when they are called beautiful. If they pretend to dislike
flattery, it is only in the hope of getting more of it. Even
when their heads are drooping with the heat, and their leaves
covered with dust, they are sorry to see the GARDENER, (*Here
Rule 4th must be observed*) for fear his WATER-POT, (*Rule 5th*)
will frighten away the crowd of insects which buzz around
them ; especially the impatient *Balsamine*."

BALSAMINE SPEAKS.

Ill-natured insect ! you waste your wit. Water is to me the
most delightful of all things, for I know it never fails to render

me more beautiful. Of what consequence is it to me that the croud of insects fly away? cannot I entice them back whenever I choose? If I open my corolla invitingly, they will come eagerly enough. When I grow weary of them, I can, by a slight contraction, fire off one of my seed-vessels,* and disperse them in the air instantly. As for the crawling things which the water washes upon the ground, do you suppose I want their company? For instance, the lazy *Caterpillar.*

CATERPILLAR SPEAKS.

I could never imagine how any of the insects could admire you. You are a vain coquette, your temper is irritable, you exhale no perfume, and you are not half as beautiful as most other flowers. I do not say these harsh things because I am angry, but because they are true. I never flatter beauties, and I do not want their smiles; but I do love to crawl where I can breathe the fragrance of one modest little flower! How can any insect prefer the gaudy coquette to the lovely, the sweet, and the timid? Tell me, my little wise and modest *Violet.*

VIOLET SPEAKS.

If insects knew what true love was, they would not seek the brightest and most showy flowers. True affection will seek

---

* The seed-vessels of the Balsamine, or Touch-me-not, burst open as soon as an insect rests upon them.

affection in return among the secluded and the diffident; but the vain are attracted by vanity: what the world praises is of more value in their eyes than real merit. Far wiser than this is the busy *Bee*.

THE BEE SPEAKS.

As we have given instances enough to explain the game, we shall leave our young readers to make what speech they please for the Bee.

HOW DO YOU LIKE IT? WHEN DO YOU LIKE IT?
AND WHERE WILL YOU PUT IT?

THE difficulty of this game consists in guessing the meaning of two or more nouns, which sound alike, but mean differently, without any other help than answers to the above questions. I will give an example. One of the company is sent out of the room, and not recalled until her companions have agreed upon words of similar sound, with which to puzzle her. When she comes in she asks, "How do you like it?" One answers, "Very much indeed;" another says, "I don't like it too early in the morning;" another says, "It is too noisy;" another says, "It is too fond of fine clothes;" &c. She then asks, "When do you like it?" One answers, "At all times;" another says, "When I feel hungry for my dinner;" another says, "I want it when walking alone;" another, "When I want some wood brought for my fire;" &c. Lastly, she asks, "Where would you put it?" One says, "I would hang it;" another, "I would shut it up in a church;" another, "I would take it to a ball room," &c.

From these answers, a witty little girl may guess that *bell* was the chosen word: *bell*, an instrument of sound, and *belle*, a fashionable lady. Those who do not guess, must pay a forfeit. Many words might be chosen for this game, such as queen and quean—rain and rein—plane and plain—vice, a tool, and vice, a crime—whip, to strike with, and whip, to eat, &c.

ALPHABETICAL COMPLIMENTS

A LITTLE girl says to her companion, I love you, A, because you are amiable; B, because you are beautiful; C, because you are careful; D, because you are diligent; E, because you are elegant; F, because you are funny; and so on to the end of the alphabet. X is of course omitted, for no English word begins with that letter. Any letter omitted, or a reason given which does not begin with the letter you name, demands a forfeit.

MR. RED-CAP.

THE children all take the name of some coloured cap; as Mr. Red-cap, Mr. Blue-cap, Mr. Yellow-cap, Mr. Green-cap, &c. A handkerchief is thrown as the signal to speak; but the one who throws it must not look at the one she means to aim at, because it is desirable to take her by surprise. If she throws it at Red-cap, she must call out, " Mr. Red-cap!" Before she can count five, Red-cap must answer, " What, I, sir?" The one who called her must answer, quick as thought, " Yes, you, sir." Red-cap replies, " Not I, sir!" The other says, " Who then, sir?" Red-cap answers, " Mr. Blue-cap!" at the same time throwing the handkerchief at the one named Blue-cap. Red-cap and Blue-cap must then repeat the same questions and answers; and Blue-cap throws it at Green-cap, or any

body else who happens to be most off her guard.   Any mistake in the proper answers, or failing to speak quick enough,
demands a forfeit.   When this is played with animation, there
is an incessant sound of " Red-cap! Blue-cap! what, I, sir ?
yes, you, sir! not I, sir! who then, sir?"

———

CRIES OF PARIS.

EACH one takes the part of some of the numerous Parisian
pedlers : one sells cherries, another cakes, another old clothes,
another eggs, &c.   They walk round the apartment, and the
moment any one is called, he must immediately sing out his
appropriate cry, as much in the tone of a pedler as he can.
The one who called then asks him for something in the way
of his trade, to which he must answer, " I have not any; ask
such an one."   For the sake of improving in French, I would
advise little girls to utter the cries of Paris in the language of
Paris; but I will give a translation for those who do not know
French.   Here are some examples to illustrate how the game
is played : the one chosen to begin the game calls out, " Marchande de poires."   The pear-merchant then immediately
sings her cry.   If she sell baked pears, she sings, " Poires
cuites au four."   (*Pears baked in the oven.*)   If they are not
cooked, she sings, " A deux liards, les Anglais."   (*English
pears, two for a halfpenny.*)   The one who called her then

asks, "Avez vous des pommes?" (*Have you any apples?*)
The marchande de poires answers, "Non; demandez-en au
porter d'eau." (*No; ask them of the water-bearer.*) As soon
as the water-bearer hears his name, he calls out, "A l'eau! a
l'eau!" (*Water! Water!*) The pear-merchant then asks,
"Avez vous de l'eau d'Arcueil?" (*Have you any water from*

Cherry-Merchant.   Umbrella-Merchant.

the fountain of Arcueil?) He answers, "Non: demandez-en
au marchande de parapluies." (*No; ask the umbrella-merchant
for some.*) The umbrella-merchant sings, "Parapluie! Parapluie!" The water-bearer then asks the umbrella-merchant,
"Avez vous des parasols?" (*Have you parasols?*) The one
addressed answers, "Non; demandez-en à la marchande de
cerises." (*No; ask the cherry-merchant.*) The cherry-mer-

chant sings, "A la douce! cerises à la douce! quatre sous la livre" (*Sweet cherries! four cents a pound.*) The umbrella-merchant asks, "Avez vous des cerises noires?" (*Have you black cherries?*) She answers, "Non; demandez-en à la marchande de bouquets!" (*No; ask them of the flower-merchant.*) The flower-merchant hearing her name, begins to

Cake-Merchant.   Flower-Merchant.

sing, "Des belles roses! achetez donc des roses!" (*Some beautiful roses! buy some roses!*) The cherry-merchant asks her, "Avez vous des oeillets?" (*Have you pinks?*) She replies, "Non; demandez-en au marchand d'habits." (*No; ask the old clothes man.*) He begins to sing, "Vieux habits! vieux galons!" (*Old clothes! old trimmings!*) The flower-girl says, "Avez vous des bonnets?" (*Have you any caps?*)

He answers, "Non; demandez-en à la marchande de marée.'
(*No ; ask the fish-woman.*) She, hearing her name, begins to
sing, "Ah! qu'il est beau le marquereau!" (*Ah! what beautiful mackerel!*) The clothes man asks, "Avez vous des
soles?" (*Have you any soles?*) She says, "Non; demandez-
en au marchande de gateaux." (*No ; ask the cake-merchant.*)
She then begins her cry, "Ils brûlent! ils sont tout chauds!"
(*They burn! they are all hot!*) The fish-woman asks, "Avez
vous des gateaux de Nanterre?" (*Have you any Nanterre
cakes?*) "Non; demandez-en à la marchande de pois." (*No ;
ask the pea-merchant.*)

These examples are sufficient to give an idea of the play.
To make it more complicated, they often ask the same pedler
for three or four different things, and he refers you to as many
other pedlers. Any pedler who forgets to utter his cry when
his name is mentioned, must pay a forfeit; and if you ask a
pedler for anything not belonging to his trade, or ask for the
same thing twice, you must pay a forfeit. The continual motions and strange tones of the criers, afford much amusement.
It is a good plan to commit a large number of cries to memory
before beginning the game; such as "Pois écossés!" (*Shelled
peas!*) "Mes gros cerneaux!" (*My great walnuts!*) "Des
bon fromages!" (*Good cheeses!*) "En voulez vous de la
salade?" (*Will you buy some salad?*) "Vieux chiffons!"
(*Old millinery!*) "Les pommes de terre!" (*Potatoes!*) The
more there are engaged in the game, the merrier it is.

THE MUSICAL ORACLE, OR MAGIC MUSIC.

ONE of the company goes out of the room, and while she is absent, it is agreed what she shall be required to do when she comes back. The person at the piano begins to play as soon as she re-enters the room; and the music is more and more lively the nearer she approaches what she is destined to do, and as she moves away from it, the sounds become fainter and fainter. Thus, if it has been agreed that the absent person shall touch the right cheek of a certain individual in the room, the nearer she approaches that person, the louder and more rapid is the music; if she raises her finger, it is still more lively; but if she touches the *left* cheek, the sound instantly dies away.

If she cannot guess exactly what they wish her to do, she must pay a forfeit.

THE PUZZLE WORD.

ONE goes out of the room; and the others agree upon a word, which she is to find out by asking questions. "Does the thing you have named fly?" "Does it walk?" "Does it sing?" "Does it speak?" "Does it grow?" &c. If she cannot ascertain the word from the definitions given, she must pay a forfeit.

THE GENTEEL LADY.

THOSE who make a mistake in this difficult game must have
a paper horn twisted fantastically, and so placed in their hair
that it will shake about at the least motion. Two mistakes
receives two horns, three mistakes three horns, &c. When
a large number of twisted papers are prepared, one begins
the game by saying to the one who stands at her right hand,
"Good morning, genteel lady, always genteel; I, a genteel
lady, always genteel, come from that genteel lady, always genteel (here she points to the left), to tell you that she owns an
eagle with a golden beak." The next one attempts to repeat
the phrase, word for word, only adding, "an eagle with golden
beak *and silver claws.*" If she make the slightest mistake in
repeating the sentence, she must have a paper horn put in her
hair; and her next neighbour takes up the phrase thus, to the
one on her right hand: "Good morning, genteel lady, always

genteel; I, a genteel lady, always genteel, come from that *horned* lady, always horned (pointing to the one on her left), to say that she has an eagle with golden beak, silver claws, and *a lace skin.*" Perhaps this one will make three mistakes before she gets through the sentence, if so, the next says, "Good morning, genteel lady, always genteel; I, a genteel lady, always genteel, come from that three horned lady, always three horned, to say that she has an eagle with a golden beak, silver claws, lace skin, and *diamond eyes.*" If she should happen to receive four horns for as many mistakes, her next neighbour would say, after repeating the first part of the sentence, "I come from the four horned lady, always four horned, to say that she has an eagle with a golden beak, silver claws, lace skin, diamond eyes, and *purple feathers.*"

Thus it goes round the circle; but the second time it goes round, it is still more difficult and more droll. By that time, the chance is everybody will have a greater or less number of horns; and those who repeat must remember exactly, or else they obtain another horn. Thus, if your left hand neighbour has two horns, you have three horns, and your right hand neighbor has four, you must say, "Good morning, four horned lady, always four horned; I, a three horned lady, always three horned, come from that two horned lady, always two horned (pointing to the left), to say that she has an eagle," &c.

By the time the game is finished, the children's heads are generally ridiculous enough. To make it more funny, the speaker sometimes pretends to cry when she calls *herself* three horned, and laughs when she calls her *neighbour* four horned. This is a French game, played both by boys and girls.

PUSS, PUSS IN THE CORNER!

THIS is a very simple game, but a very lively and amusing one. In each corner of the room, or by four trees which form nearly a square, a little girl is stationed; another one stands in the centre, who is called the Puss. At the words, "Puss, puss in the corner!" they all start and run to change corners; and at the same time the one in the middle runs to take possession of the corner before the others can reach it. If she succeed in getting to the corner first, the one who is left out is obliged to become the puss. If A and B undertake to exchange corners, and A gets into B's corner, but puss gets into A's, then B must stand in the centre. In order to avoid confusion and knocking each other down, it is well to agree in what direction you will run, before the race begins. If a little girl remains puss after three or four times going round the room, they sometimes agree that she shall pay a forfeit.

THE BIRD-SELLER.

THE company are seated in a circle, one only standing in the centre, and she is called the bird-seller. She stoops down to each one, and they whisper in her ear the name of whatever bird they choose to take for themselves. These she must carefully remember. If she fears she shall forget them, she must write them with a pencil. Then she must repeat them aloud, thus: "Gentlemen and ladies, I have in my collection an Eagle, a Swan, a Bird of Paradise, a Crow, a Wren, a Magpie," &c. &c. If the lists are written down, she must be careful not to read them in the same succession she wrote them; if she does, the players will easily conjecture to whom the name belongs, and that would not be fair. After the list is read, the Bird-seller must ask each one, "To which of my birds will you make your bow? To which will you tell a secret? From which will you pluck a feather?" Each one replies according to her taste; perhaps she will answer, "I will bow to the Eagle, tell my secret to the Bird of Paradise, and pluck a feather from the Jay." Those who happen to have a feather plucked from them, must pay a forfeit; the one to whom a secret is to be imparted, has something whispered in her ear; and a bow is made where a bow is promised; little girls sometimes substitute a courtesy for a bow, when there are no boys in the game. No one must make her bow, or tell a secret, or pluck a feather, from the bird whose name she has chosen for herself. A forfeit must be paid, if any one names a bird that is not in the list. The forfeits are not paid, and the bows are not made, &c. until the Bird-seller has asked her questions all round the circle; if she cannot then remember what each one has chosen, they must put her in mind of it. If one escapes without having a feather plucked, she becomes the Bird-seller of the next game. If nobody is lucky enough to escape, the one who sat at the right hand of the Bird-seller, before she rose, is chosen.

THE ELEMENTS.

In this game the party sit in a circle; one throws a handkerchief at another, and calls out, "Air!" The person whom the handkerchief hits, must name some creature that belongs in the air, before the caller can count ten, which he does in a loud voice, and as fast as possible. If a creature that does not live in the air is named, or if the person fails to speak quick enough, a forfeit must be paid. The person who catches the handkerchief throws it to another, in turn, and calls out, "Earth!" The person who is hit must call out elephant, or ox, or any creature which lives upon the earth, in the same space of time allowed the other. She then throws the handkerchief to another, and calls out, "Water!" The one who catches the handkerchief observes the same rules as the preceding, and is liable to the same forfeits. Any one who mentions a bird, beast, or fish, twice, is likewise liable to a forfeit. If any one player calls out, "Fire!" every one must keep silence, because no creature lives in that element.

THE FRENCH ROLL.

In the beginning, some one is chosen to perform the part of *purchaser*. She stands apart, while the others arrange themselves in a long file, one behind the other, each taking hold of her neighbour's sleeve. The little girl who happens to be at the head is a *baker*; all the others form the *oven*, with the exception of the last one, who is called the French Roll. The *baker* does not keep her station long, as you will see. As soon as the file is formed, the *purchaser* comes up to the *baker*, and says, "Give me my roll." The baker answers, "It is behind the oven." The purchaser goes in search of it, and at the same moment the little girl at the end, who is called the roll, lets go her companion's sleeve, and runs up on the side opposite the purchaser, crying when she starts, "Who runs? who runs?" Her object is to get in front of the baker before the purchaser can catch her. If she succeed, she becomes baker, and the little girl who stood next above her becomes the roll; if she does not succeed, she has to take the place of the purchaser, and the purchaser becomes baker. This play is a very active, and rather a noisy, one. When the company get fully engaged in it, there is nothing heard but "Give me my roll!" "It is behind the oven." "Who runs? who runs?" As they do not run very far, they can run very quick, without fatigue; and as they are changing places all the time, each one has a share of the game. Sometimes they make it a rule, that every one who is caught in trying to get before the baker, shall pay a forfeit; but when they stop to pay forfeits, the game is not so animated.

THE COMICAL CONCERT.

This game, when well played, is extremely diverting. The players stand in a circle, and each one agrees to imitate some instrument of music. One pretends to play upon the violin, by holding out her right hand, and moving her left as if she were drawing a bow across it. *Those who have seen Mr. Maelzel's little fiddler, will know how to do this to perfection.* Another doubles up her two hands, and puts them to her mouth, to imitate a horn; another moves her fingers on a table, as if she were playing the piano; another takes the back of a chair, and touches the rounds, as if they were the strings of a harp; another makes motions as if beating a drum; another holds a stick after the manner of a guitar, and pretends to play upon it; another appears to be turning a

3

hand-organ; in a word, the players, if sufficiently numerous, may imitate every instrument they ever heard of. This is but half the game. Each musician, while playing, must make a sound with her mouth in imitation of her instrument, thus:

> Rub-a-dub goes the drum.
> Twang, twang, goes the harp.
> Toot, too hoo, goes the horn.
> Tweedle dee, tweedle dee, goes the violin, &c.

All this makes an odd jumble of movements and sounds, which is very laughable, especially if each one plays her part with animation.

In the middle of the circle stands one called the *head of the orchestra*, whose business it is to beat time to the movements of the rest, which she does in as ridiculous a way as possible, in order to make the others laugh. In the midst of all the noise and fun, she suddenly stops, and asks abruptly, "Why don't you play better?" The one she looks at must answer *instantly*, in a manner suitable to the nature of her instrument; that is, the drummer must say one of the drumsticks is broken; the harper, that the strings are too loose; the person playing on the piano must say one of the dampers is broken, or one of the keys makes a discord; the flute player, that the holes are too far apart for her fingers, &c.

If they hesitate a moment, or the answer is not such as is suitable to the instrument, or if they repeat an excuse that has been already made, they must pay a forfeit. While one is answering, the others stop playing; and all begin again as soon as she has said her say, or paid her forfeit. Then the head of the orchestra looks at some other one, and asks why she don't play better; and so it goes on till they are weary of the game. Sometimes they make it a rule, that any one who laughs so that she cannot play her part, must pay a forfeit; in this case there would be plenty of forfeits.

FLY AWAY, PIGEON!

The company are ranged in a circle, with one in the centre, who places the fore-finger of her right hand upon her knee and all the others put their fore-fingers around it. If the one in the centre raises her finger, saying, at the same instant, "Fly away, pigeon!" or "Fly away, sparrow!" the others must raise their fingers in the same manner; but if, for the sake of mischief, she exclaims, "Fly away, trout!" or "Fly away, elephant!" the others must be careful not to move their fingers, else they must pay a forfeit. That is, the fingers must all rise, if a creature is mentioned that *can* fly; and kept quiet, if a thing which *cannot* fly is named. As it is done with great rapidity, it requires quick ears and quick thoughts. Sometimes things which fly only by accident are mentioned; such as a feather, a leaf, a sheet of paper, thistle-down, a veil, &c. In this case, all the players never make up their minds soon enough; some fingers will rise, and some keep still; and often debates will arise to determine which is right. "I am sure a leaf don't fly," says one; "I am sure it does fly on the wind," says another, &c. The one in the centre decides all disputed questions. This game brings laughing and forfeits in abundance.

THE FLYING FEATHER.

A CIRCLE amuse themselves by blowing one to the other, a feather, a light tuft of unspun cotton, or silk; in a word, any thing that is light enough to be kept up by the breath. Each one is anxious to pass it to her neighbour; because if it falls upon the floor, or upon her own clothes, she must pay a forfeit. Sometimes it is blown too violently, and it will fly so high that the next person must stretch out her neck in order to get a puff at it; at other times the breath is so feeble, that the feather will descend; sometimes it flies sideways, or behind the circle, so that one must turn her head very suddenly to catch it. It looks very droll to see a whole circle turning, and twisting, and puffing, to keep up one poor little feather.

THE OX-FOOT.

NINE people are ranged in a circle. One places his hand upon his knee; the next places her hand on the top of his hand; the next does the same to her; and so on until there is a pile of nine hands. The one whose hand is lowest then draws it out, and places it on the top, calling out, "One!" The next lowest does the same, calling out, "Two!" and so on until one cries, "Nine!" This last player must catch one of the hands beneath her, if she can, exclaiming, "Nine! I hold my ox-foot!" But as all the players know that the ninth one has a right to catch them, they try hard to withdraw their hands too quick for her. Whoever is made prisoner, must pay a forfeit. This game, to be amusing, needs to be done very rapidly. Some other phrase might be chosen instead of "I hold my ox-foot!" such as, "I've caught the weasel!"

THE SALE OF THE OX-FOOT.

THE players are seated in a circle, except one who stands in the centre, and is called the Ox-foot Merchant. Holding out a key, or a penknife, or whatever happens to be convenient, he says to one of the company, "How much will you give me for my ox-foot?" The one who is addressed takes the key and answers immediately what he will give; but he must pay a forfeit if he say nine, or any figure made by multiplying nine. He must not say nineteen, nor twenty-nine; neither must he say eighteen, because it is twice nine; nor twenty-seven, because it is three times nine. The one who buys the key moves into the centre, and the first merchant seats himself in his place; thus there is a continual change, and every one takes his turn. The one who has just sold the key, must not be asked how much he will give for it, until it has been two or three times round; that is, he must not be immediately asked, before he has time to collect his thoughts. The answers should be given very promptly; if there is any hesitation, the play becomes very tiresome. Sometimes the merchant, in order to bewilder his customers, will look at one, as if he were going to offer the key to her, and then suddenly turn round to another who is thinking nothing about it.

As the game goes on, forfeits multiply; for no price must be mentioned that has been already named.

BUZ!

This is a very lively and interesting game. Any number of children excepting seven, both boys and girls, seat themselves round a table, or in a circle. One begins the game by saying, "One!" the little girl to the left says, "Two!" and so it goes round till it arrives at *seven*, which number must not be mentioned, but in place thereof the word "Buz!" Wherever the number seven occurs, or any number into which seven may be multiplied, "Buz!" must be used instead of that number. Such are the numbers 7, 14, 17, 21, 27, 28, 35, 37, &c. &c. Any one mentioning any number with seven in it instead of "Buz!" or calling out of her turn, or naming a wrong number, must pay a forfeit. After she has paid her forfeit, she calls out, "One!" and so it goes round again to the left, by which means each has to say a different number. When by a little practice the circle get as high as seventy-one, then "Buz-one!" "Buz-two!" &c. must be used; and for seventy-seven, "Buz-buz!" and so on. If the person whose turn it is to speak delays longer than while any one of the circle can moderately count five, she must pay a forfeit.

THE HEN-COOP.

LITTLE girls amuse themselves a good deal with this game. In this country, I believe it is called "Making Cheeses;" but in France they call it the Hen-Coop. It consists in spinning round to the right rapidly for a minute; then stopping very suddenly, at the same moment bending the limbs a little, and extending the arms, in order to balance the body. The gown, inflated by the wind, will stand out in the shape of a hen-coop; therefore I think the French name is the most appropriate. After the little girl has paused a minute, she spins round to the left, and produces the same effect. Sometimes a great many play it together. One, who stands apart, claps her hands as a signal for them to begin; and if they all keep time in whirling round, and all form their hen-coops at once, it makes a very pretty sort of dance. Those who do not succeed in making a hen-coop, or who do not form it till the others have done, must pay a forfeit. The girl who gives the signal, and who is called the *chicken*, decides about this. Sometimes half of a company will play, while the other half .ook on and judge the game. In this case, the chickens and the hen-coops take turns.

WHERE IS PRETTY MARGARET?

THIS is not unlike the last. One little girl kneels down in the centre of a circle, while her companions raise her robe over her head, and hold it in such a way that it resembles a hen-coop bottom upwards. The gown is called *the Tower*, and the little girls who hold it are called *Stones*. One stands apart from the circle, and is called *the Enemy*. When the game begins, the enemy comes up and sings, " Where is pretty Margaret ? Where is pretty Margaret gone ?" The one who is kneeling answers, " She is shut up in her tower." The enemy asks, "Cannot I come in ?" The stones reply, " No, you must carry away the tower." The enemy takes one little girl by the hand, and leads her away, saying, " Won't it do to take away one stone ?" They answer, " No, you must take the whole tower." He then leads away the second, and asks, "Will not two stones do ?" He receives the same reply. Then he leads away a third and a fourth, after the same fashion, until finally there is but one remains : she holds the gown folded in her hands, and as soon as the enemy turns from her, she drops it on the head of pretty Margaret, and runs. Margaret jumps up and runs after her. They all join in the chase ; and the first one the enemy can catch, must take his place for the next game. Any one that gets caught before they have run round the room once, pays a forfeit.

HOLD FAST! AND LET GO!

Four little girls each hold the corner of a handkerchief. One standing by says, " Hold fast !" and then they must all drop the corners they are holding. When she says, " Let go !" they must be sure and keep hold. Those who fail to do this, must pay a forfeit.

THUS SAYS THE GRAND MUFTI!

This is a favourite game among children. One stands up in a chair, who is called the " Grand Mufti." He makes whatever motion he pleases, such as putting his hand on his heart, stretching out his arm, smiting his forehead, making up a sorrowful face, &c. At each motion he says, " Thus says the

Grand Mufti!" or, " So says the Grand Mufti!" When he says, " *Thus* says the Grand Mufti!" every one must make just such a motion as he does; but when he says, " *So* says the Grand Mufti!" every one must keep still. A forfeit for a mistake.

—

HUNT THE SLIPPER.

ALL the players but one are placed in a circle; that one remains outside to hunt the slipper, which is passed from hand to hand very rapidly in the circle. The hunter cannot judge where it is, because all the players keep their hands moving all the time, as if they were passing it. The one in whose hands it is caught becomes the hunter, and pays a forfeit. Usually, I believe, little girls play it sitting side by side, very close to each other, on low stools, or resting upon their feet. If the company is sufficiently numerous, it is better to have two circles, one within another, sitting face to face, resting on their feet, with their knees bent forward so as to meet each other; in this way a sort of concealed arch is formed, through which the slipper may be passed unperceived. There should be two slight openings in the circle, one on one side, and the other opposite. When the slipper is passing through these openings, the player who passes it should tap it on the floor, to let the hunter know where it is. She springs to seize it; but it is flying round so rapidly, and all hands are moving so fast, that she loses it, and in less than an instant, perhaps, she hears it tapping on the other side. This game may be played rudely, and it may be played politely. If little girls are rude, they are in great danger of knocking each other down in try ing to catch the slipper: for squatting upon their feet, as they do in this game, they easily lose their balance. It is best for the hunter never to try to catch the slipper except at the two openings in the circle; then there is no danger of tumbling each other down. Some prefer playing this game with a thimble or a marble, because it is not so likely to be seen as a slipper. If any one happens to drop the slipper in passing it, she must pay a forfeit.

HUNT THE RING.

ALL the company are seated in a circle, each one holding a ribbon which passes all round. An ivory ring is slipped along the ribbon; and while all hands are in motion, the hunter in the centre must find where it is, if he can. The one with whom it is caught becomes the hunter.

KING GEORGE'S TROOPS.

Two little girls stand with their arms raised, so as to form an arch. The rest of the company arrange themselves in a file, each taking hold of the next one's gown: in this manner they pass through the arch, singing,

"Open the gates sky high,
And let King George's troops pass by !"

By suddenly lowering the arches, the last one is caught; and unless she answers promptly any question put to her, she must pay a forfeit.

JUDGE AND JURY.

A CIRCLE is formed, at the head of which are placed three on elevated seats, called the Judge and Jury. Before the game begins, all except these three have some name or other assigned them. Thus one will be called necklace, another bracelets, another sash, and so on. A tin or wooden plate lies in the centre. When the judge says, " My lady is going out, and wants her necklace," the one named necklace must jump up, and spin the plate round like a top. But there are certain rules to be observed in doing this, which are extremely difficult. She must not make any motion, without first asking leave of the judge. She must say, " May I get up?" " May I walk?" " May I stoop?" " May I pick up the plate?" " May I spin it?" " Shall I break it, or shall I place it?" (By breaking it, she merely means letting it fall bottom-upwards.) If she is told to break it, and it does not happen to fall that way, she must forfeit. After the plate stops, she cannot return without first asking, " May I walk?" " May I sit down?" A forfeit is paid for every instance of forgetfulness in these rules. The judge proclaims the forfeits; and after the circle have all tried their luck, the jury go out of the room to decide in what manner they shall be paid. I forgot to mention that they do not rise in succession: they wait for the judge to say, " My lady wants her sash, or her bracelets," &c.

BUFF SAYS BUFF TO ALL HIS MEN.

THIS game, like many others, is merely a way of collecting forfeits. The company are seated in a circle; one holds a little stick in her hand, and says,

> "Buff says buff to all his men,
> And I say buff to you again;
> Buff neither laughs nor smiles—
> But carries his face
> With a very good grace,
> And passes his stick to the very next place."

As she concludes, she holds the stick to the one next her, who takes it, and repeats the same; and so on, in succession. Those who laugh or smile, while saying it, must pay a forfeit.

WHO WILL BUY A BIRD'S NEST?

IN this play it is of no consequence how the company are seated. One goes round and asks, "Who buys my bird's nest ?"   If any one answers, " I will," she says, " What will you give for it ?"   The answers given will be various—some will give a straw, others a sugar-plum, others a cent, &c. After all have told what they will give for the bird's nest, the seller has a right to ask each one six questions, which they must answer without laughing, or pay a forfeit.   These questions may be made as ridiculous as possible, but they ought to relate either to the bird's nest, or the price that is offered for it; such as, " What shall I do with a straw ?"   " Shall I keep it to suck cider ?"   " Shall I make a mouse's bonnet of it ?" " Shall I tickle a rat's ear with it ?"   &c.

The nest of a Tailor-Bird—so called because she sews .eaves together with strong grass.

THE SHEPHERD AND THE WOLF.

THE company stand in a file, holding by each other's dresses, and are called lambs; one little girl at the head is called the shepherdess; one stands outside, and is called the wolf. As the latter walks round, the shepherdess calls out, "Who is round my house this dark night?" The one on the outside answers, "A wolf! a wolf!" The shepherdess says, "Let my lambs alone." The wolf answers, "There is one little one I will take," at the same time trying to take away the little girl at the bottom of the file. The shepherdess springs forward to stop her; the lambs all follow the motion of the shepherdess; the wolf tries to profit by the general confusion—she pretends to jump to the left, and then suddenly darts to the right. If any one gets caught, she must pay a forfeit. Sometimes one gets caught, and slips away; in that case she must run and place herself before the shepherdess for safety. When this happens, she must take upon herself the troublesome employment of the shepherdess; the wolf, likewise, loses her place, and pays a forfeit. The last lamb in the file takes the place of the wolf.

THE CAT AND THE MOUSE.

ALL the company stand hand in hand, in a circle; one is placed inside, called the mouse; another outside, called the cat. They begin by turning round rapidly, raising their arms; the cat springs in at one side, and the mouse jumps out at the other; they then suddenly lower their arms, so that the cat cannot escape. The cat goes round mi-au-ing, trying to get out: and as the circle are obliged to keep dancing round all the time, she will find a weak place to break through, if she is a sharp-sighted cat. As soon as she gets out, she chases the mouse, who tries to save herself by getting within the circle again. For this purpose, they raise their arms; if she gets in without being followed by the cat, the cat must pay a forfeit, and try again; but if the mouse is caught, she must pay a forfeit. Then they name who shall succeed them; they fall into the circle, and the game goes on.

OLD MAN IN HIS CASTLE.

A LINE is drawn on the floor, or a large crack chosen as a boundary; one stands on one side of the line, and all the others are ranged on the opposite side. By and by, one ventures over, and asks, " May I have some of your apples, old man ?" The moment the line is crossed, he darts forward exclaiming, "Go off my grounds!" If he can catch the culprit on his own grounds, she is obliged to take his place; but he has no right to go over the line in the pursuit. Sometimes three or four intruders will be in at once. Children vary the questions as they please: sometimes they ask for cherries. or birds, or hay, or blackberries.

HUNT THE SQUIRREL.

ALL the company, except one, form into a circle, that one remains outside, walking round and round with a handkerchief in her hand. Presently she drops it; and the one at whose feet it falls must dart forward to catch the squirrel that has dropped the handkerchief. While running, she must sing, "Hunt the squirrel through the wood! Now I've lost him— now I've found him! Hunt the squirrel through the wood!"

If the game is played well, it is very lively and amusing. The little girls all keep an eye upon the squirrel, as she walks round, eager to see where the handkerchief will fall; but if she is cunning, she will try to drop it behind some one who is least on the watch, in order that she may have time to get the start in the chase. While running, the squirrel zig-zags in all manner of directions, dodging in and dodging out, so as to puzzle her pursuer as much as she can. When caught, the pursuer becomes the squirrel.

HUNT THE WHISTLE.

A KEY, or something similar, is used for this game, and is called the whistle. The one in the centre of the circle must be ignorant of the game, or else the fun is all lost. Those who compose the circle keep their hands in motion all the time, as if they were passing the whistle, in the same manner they do in Hunt the Slipper; and frequently some one whistles, to make the hunter think it is passing through their hands at that instant. But, in fact, some one before the game begins manages to fasten the string of the key, either with a pin or a button, upon the back of the hunter herself. It makes a great laugh to see it whirling round her, as she turns at every whistle. But I don't like this game very well. There is deception in it; and even in play all should be fair.

———

TIERCÉ, OR TOUCH THE THIRD.

IN this game the company stand two and two in a circle excepting in one place, where they stand three deep, thus:

One stands outside of the circle, and is on no account allowed to go within it. The object is to touch the *third* one, wherever he finds her; but when he attempts this, she darts into the circle, and takes her place before some of the others. Then the third one who stands behind her becomes the object; but she likewise slips into the circle, and takes her place in front of another. The pursuer is thus led from point to point in the circle, for he must always aim at one who forms the outside of a row of three. Any one caught, changes places with the pursuer. This game affords charming exercise. Sometimes they agree that the pursuer may touch the third one with his handkerchief—which he is of course more likely to effect than by touching with his hand.

———

SEE-SAW.

This consists in riding on a board, placed across a block of wood or a low fence. The block must not be placed in the middle, but much nearer one end than the other. A little girl seats herself on one end, and her companion on the other. As one rises, the other sinks; and thus a constant and pleasing motion is obtained. Care should be taken to have the board securely placed.

TWINE THE GARLAND, GIRLS!

THIS is a simple kind of dance. A line of young ladies take hold of each other's hands: one stands perfectly still, while the others dance round her, winding and stopping—winding and stopping—until they are all formed into a knot. Then they gradually untwist in the same manner. As they form the knot, they sing, "Twine the garland, girls!" and when they unwind, they sing, "Untwine the garland, girls!"

WASH MY LADY'S DRESSES.

THIS somewhat resembles a dance. Two stand face to face, each laying her right hand upon the left hand of the other. They swing their arms, slowly and gracefully, first to the right side, then to the left, three times each way, singing, "Wash my lady's dresses! Wash my lady's dresses!" They then part; each one places the palms of her hands together, and moves them up and down three times, to imitate the motion of rinsing clothes, singing all the time, "Rinse them out! Rinse them out!" The next motion is much prettier. They take hold of hands as in the beginning; the arms on one side, are raised so as to form an arch; each one stoops, and passes the head under; this brings them back to back. The arms on the other side are then raised, and the heads passed through; this brings them again face to face. This should be done very rapidly, singing all the time, "Wring them out! Wring them out!" After this motion has been repeated three times, they stop suddenly, and clap hands thrice, singing, "And hang them on the bushes!" Where this is played by several couples, who keep time with each other, it is very graceful and animated.

———

I SPY!

THIS game is usually played out of doors; because more convenient hiding-places are to be found there. All the company hide, except one; who is kept blinded, until she hears them call, "Whoop!" She then takes the bandage from her eyes, and begins to search for them. If she catches a glimpse of any one, and knows who it is, she calls her by name, " I spy Harriet!" or "I spy Mary!" The one who is thus discovered, must start and run for the place where the other was first blinded. If she do not reach the spot, without being touched by her pursuer, she must take her place.

JACOB! WHERE ARE YOU?

THIS game is very similar to Blind Man's Buff. One of the company is blindfolded; after which one of the little girls takes a bell and joins the rest of her companions. The one who jingles the bell is called Jacob; the blindfolded one goes round, saying "Jacob! where are you?" In answer to which Jacob jingles the bell. The blinded one follows the sound; but Jacob dodges about in every direction—sometimes at the farthest corner of the room,—sometimes impudently shaking her bell in the very ear of her pursuer. If caught, they change places.

———

HIDE AND GO SEEK!

ONE goes out of the room, while the others hide a thimble, pocket handkerchief, or something of that sort. When they are ready, they call "Whoop!" and she enters. If she moves toward the place, they cry, "You burn!" "Now you burn more!" If she goes very near, they say, "Oh! you are almost blazing!" If she moves from the object, they say, "How cold she grows!" If the article is found, the one who hid it must take the next turn to seek for it.

BLIND MAN'S BUFF.

THE ancient game is so well known that it needs but a brief notice. One of the company is blinded, and runs round to catch the others, who all try to keep out of his grasp, at the same time that they go as near him as they can. If he catches one, and cannot tell who it is, he must let her go, and try again. Sometimes a forfeit is paid in this case; but all the varieties of blind man's buff are usually played without forfeits. One fairly caught and known, must take the blind man's place.

———

SHADOW BUFF.

THIS is the best kind to play in winter's evenings. It is so safe and quiet that it disturbs no one: and good little girls will never play noisy games, without first ascertaining whether it will be pleasant to parents and friends. Thinking of the wishes and feelings of others, even in the most trifling things constitutes true politeness; and those, who are habitually polite at home, will be so when they are abroad without any effort.

Shadow Buff is played in the following manner; if the window happen to have a white curtain, it may be fastened at the bottom, so as to make a smooth still surface; in the absence of a white curtain, a table-cloth may be fastened upon the wall. The one chosen to act the part of the blind man sits before the curtain, with his back to the light and to his companions. When all is arranged, they pass by on the opposite side of the room, so as to cast their shadows on the white surface. They may put on turbans, or shawls, or walk lame, or anything else to disguise themselves; and he must tell who they are, if he can.

FETTERED BUFF.

In this play no one is blinded; but one is required to catch the others with his wrists tied behind him.   This is the least interesting form of Blind Man's Buff.

———

BLIND MAN'S WAND.

This is a variety of the same game.   The blinded man carries a little stick or cane, which he reaches out in every direction.   Whoever it touches, is bound by the laws of the game to take hold of it, and repeat whatever the blind man orders.   The one who is caught may disguise his voice as he pleases; and he cannot be required to say more than three things.   If the blind man cannot find him out by his voice he must try again.

CHINESE SHADOWS.

CHILDREN are generally extremely fond of this play.   It can be played only in the evening, by candle-light, and in a room with large curtains ; white curtains are the best.   In order to fasten the curtain tight, so as to render it smooth and motion-less, it should be let down and fastened to the wall with pins on each side.   Half the children may be spectators, and the other half actors.   The spectators should be seated in rows, facing the curtain.   Those in the foremost row should hold a ribbond or little stick, across the curtain, as high as their arms can conveniently reach, in order to mark out the ground on which the shadows are to move.   The actors should stand be-hind the spectators, at a little distance, with an ample provision of figures cut in paper; such as houses, trees, men, women, animals, &c.   These figures must be made to pass slowly one after another, in such a manner as you wish the shadows to be thrown upon the curtain.   It is easy to make these figures advance, retreat, meet each other, &c. while you hold a con-versation for them.   Some who are skilful in the management of these shadows, can make them represent a battle, blind-man's buff, a contra-dance, &c.   The houses, trees, and other inanimate things, must not of course be moved ; birds must be suspended on the ends of several strings, and swung about irregularly, from time to time.   The effect is not unlike a magic lantern.   When the actors have played long enough, they must change places with the spectators.

FRENCH AND ENGLISH.

This game being merely a trial of strength, may be thought unsuitable to little girls; but I know that families of brothers and sisters are very fond of it. It consists of two parties, whose numbers are equal. A line is drawn on the ground, or on the floor, and the object of each of these parties is to draw the other entirely over it. When every one is drawn over, the other side call them prisoners, and claim a victory. Those who join hands in the centre, should be very careful not to let go suddenly; for this would be sure to occasion violent and dangerous falls.

HERE I BAKE, AND HERE I BREW.

A CIRCLE of girls hold each other firmly by the hand; one in the centre, touches one pair of hands, saying, "Here I bake;" another, saying, "Here I brew;" another saying, "Here I make my wedding-cake;" another, saying, "Here I mean to break through." As she says the last phrase she pushes hard, to separate their hands; if she succeed, the one whose hand gave way takes her place; if not, she keeps going the rounds till she can break through. Sometimes they exact a forfeit from any one who tries three times without success; but it is usually played without forfeits.

———

YOU ARE NOTHING BUT A GOOSE

THIS play consists in telling a story, and at the same time making marks to illustrate what you are telling. For instance: An old man and his wife lived in a little round cabin. I will sketch it for you with my pencil, so that you may know it. Here it is : O   This cabin had a window in the middle, which I shall make thus : o   On one side was a projecting door, which I shall make opposite the window thus : =   From the side opposite the door branched out a road, bordered on one side with a hedge. Here is a picture of it : ⟍⟍   This road terminated in a large pond. Here it is : ⟋‾‾‾⟍   Herbs grew around it, which I mark thus :  One night some robbers came to the farther end of this pond. I will mark them thus : The old woman heard them, and persuaded her husband to get up and see what was the matter. The old people travelled along down to about the middle of the pond, and there they stopped ; I shall represent them thus : / | Each one held out a hand to keep silence, which movement I shall make thus : ⌒ ⌒

But they did not hear anything ; for the robbers had taken fright and run away. After standing out in the cold some time for nothing, the old man said to his wife, " Go along back to the house ; *you are nothing but a goose.*" As you say these words, hold up the sheet of paper on which you have been drawing, and the company will see the picture of a goose rudely sketched thus :

While making your marks, you must be careful that those who are watching you see the picture sideways, or upside down ; otherwise they will be apt to suspect your design before you finish it.

THE PUZZLE WALL.

SUPPOSE there was a pond, around which four poor men built their houses, thus :

Suppose four wicked rich men afterwards built houses around the poor people, thus :

and wished to have all the water of the pond to themselves. How could they build a high wall, so as to shut out the poor people from the pond?   You might try on your slate a great while, and not do it.   I will show you.

THE CRADLE OF LOVE.

THIS little game has exercise and graceful movement to recommend it. All, except two, take their places as in a contra-dance; the two who are thus left out join hands, and attempt to dance between the couple at the foot; the couple join hands and inclose them; and the prisoners are not allowed to escape, till each has turned round and kissed the one behind her. In this way they dance through every couple in the set. When performed with ease and animation, it is very pleasing. Sometimes this is used as a forfeit.

———

WHIRLIGIGS.

THESE are made by fastening a button-mould on a peg, or large pin, and spinning them round on the table, or on the floor. The peg or pin should be fastened firmly through the centre of the mould, come out a little at one end, and be left half an inch long, or more, at the other. If a number of little girls prepare them of different sizes and colours, they look very prettily when they are all in rapid motion.

5

LEAP, FROG, LEAP!

A CIRCLE of little girls squat upon their feet, with their clothes carefully gathered around them, so as not to entangle them when they jump; in this fashion they try to hop round after each other, like a company of frogs—singing all the while, "Leap, frog, leap!" They cannot play this long; for the unnatural and awkward posture perplexes and fatigues them. This game would appear ridiculous in any except very young children.

PAT A CAKE.

THIS is a common diversion for infants all the world over. Clap the hands together, saying, "Pat a cake, pat a cake, baker's man; that I will, master, as fast as I can;" then rub the hands together, saying, "Roll it, and roll it;" then peck the palm of the left hand with the fore-finger of the right, saying "Prick it, and prick it;" then throw up both hands, saying, "Toss it in the oven and bake it."

Pat a cake, pat a cake, baker's man!
Bake me a cake as fast as you can;
Roll it, and prick it, and mark it with T,
Toss it in the oven for Thomas and me

SOAP BUBBLES.

THIS simple amusement gives great delight to children, who love dearly to watch the splendid rainbow colours of the bubbles as they rise. A bowl of foaming suds, and a piece of pipe-stem, or straw, or quill, is all that is necessary. Some think that the bubbles are much larger if the quill, or straw, be soaked a little at the end which you apply to the suds, and split into four, about the length of your nail. If you cannot blow the bubble to such size as you wish, do not try to increase it by taking in more suds: for the moment it touches the water, it will burst. When the bubble is formed, shake the pipe, and it will rise and float in the air, looking like a piece of the rainbow

THE ONE-FOOTED CHACE.

LITTLE girls often amuse themselves with trying who can jump farthest on one foot, while the other is bent, and raised and sometimes one jumping ·in this manner, tries to catch her companions, who all hop along in the same manner.

———

JACK STRAWS.

A LARGE number of straws, or fine splinters of wood, of equal length, are placed in a pile, standing up so as to meet at the top and spread out at the bottom, like a tent, or hay-stack; two of the sticks are reserved, and on these are placed little crooked pins, or some small delicate kind of hook. Each one, in turn, takes these hooks and tries to remove one from the pile, without shaking any other straw. The one who succeeds in removing a straw upon these difficult conditions, takes it to herself, and counts one. Those who gain the most straws win the game. Sometimes they cut little notches, or they black the heads of three, which they call king, queen, and bishop. the king counts four, the queen three, and the bishop two

BOB CHERRY.

ONE in the centre holds a cherry; while each one tries to catch it in her mouth. This simple game must be played with great good humour; if any crying or disputing begins, the play should stop at once.

———

THE CUP OF SAND.

THIS is similar to Jack Straws. A little stick with a flag upon it is placed in a cup heaping full of sand. Each child tries to knock out a little sand, without making the standard fall. The one at whose touch it falls, must rise and make a bow, or a courtesy, to each of the others.

RABBIT ON THE WALL.

WHEN older sisters have the care of very young ones, there are a variety of ways to keep them quiet and happy. In the evening, when shadows can be cast on the wall, nothing pleases them more than rabbits' and foxes' heads, made on the wall by holding the hands thus:

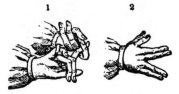

1 is the rabbit; 2 is the fox. If the second and third fingers are kept moving towards each other in No. 2, it will look as if the fox were eating.

———

FLY AWAY, JACK!

A MORSEL of wet paper, or a wafer, is put upon the nails of your two middle fingers. You rest these two fingers only, side by side, upon the edge of a table; naming one Jack, and the other Gill. You raise one suddenly, exclaiming, "Fly away Jack!" When you bring the hand down again, hide your middle finger, and place your fore-finger on the table. Then raise the other, saying, " Fly away, Gill !" and bring down your fore-finger instead of your middle one. Then the papers have disappeared; and if you do it quick, your companions will think the birds have flown. Then raise your hand and cry, " Come again, Jack ;" bring the middle finger down, and the paper is again seen. Then bid Gill come again in the same manner.

DANCE, BUMPKIN, DANCE!

ANOTHER species of amusement on these occasions is to hold up the hand, bending thumb and fingers; keep the thumb in motion for a while, singing in a lively tone, " Dance, bumpkin, dance !" Then keep the thumb still, and move the fore fingers, singing, " Dance, ye merry men, every one ! for bumpkin, he can dance alone." Then move the fore-finger, and sing, " Dance, foreman, dance !" Then move all the fingers, singing, " Dance, ye merry men, every one ! for foreman, he can dance alone." Then keep the second finger in motion and sing, "Dance, middle-man, dance !" Then move all the fingers, singing, "Dance, ye merry men, one and all! for middle-man, he can dance alone." Then in the same manner repeat the process with the two other fingers; calling the third finger ring-man, and the fourth finger little-man. When these changes are done rapidly, it makes babies laugh very much.

THIS LITTLE PIG WENT TO MARKET.

THIS is the most common of all plays for infants. Touch the thumb, saying, "This little pig went to market;" touch the fore-finger, saying, "This little pig staid at home;" to the middle finger, "This little pig had roast meat;" to the fourth finger, "This little pig had none;" to the little finger, "This little pig cries squeak! squeak!"

Sometimes they say the following words: "This little pig says, I want wheat;" "This little pig says, where will you get it?" "This little pig says, in father's barn;" "This little pig says, I can't get over the door-sill;" "This little pig cries, squeak! squeak!"

————

BUY MY GEESE.

THE little finger is doubled over the second finger; the middle finger over the fore-finger; and twisted thus, they all rest upon the thumb. You then ask, "Will you buy my geese?" If they say, "Yes," suddenly untwist your fingers, exclaiming, "Ah, they have all flown away!"

————

BO, PEEP!

A VERY little girl can amuse her baby-brother or sister by this play. It consists merely in hiding one's head for a moment, and then popping it out, singing, "Bo, peep!"

SILVER SOUND.

PLACE your right hand inside your left, and let the fingers and thumb of the left hand clasp it gently; then ask, " What have I got in my hand?" at the same time striking the back of your left hand against your knee. The person asked will say, " Silver money;" for the sound is exactly like two pieces of money striking against each other. Then open your hands and shew them there is nothing there.

CARD HOUSES.

THE prettiest way of making these is to put two cards together, touching at the top, and spread at the bottom, like a tent; place four of these close to each other; upon the top of all of them lay a couple of cards flat, to form a new floor; on the floor place three more little tents; then make another floor of cards laid flat; then put two little tents; then another floor, then one tent. Here you must stop; for a new floor will not rest on one point. If you can have a whole table to yourself, you can make a fence all around it, by making cards stand in and out, resting against each other, like a Virginia fence; other little tents standing about may represent barns, summer-houses, &c. And if you have any little wooden dogs, cows, milk-maids, &c. you can make it look quite like a little farm-house.

HEADS OR POINTS.

LITTLE girls often hold two pins in their hands, and ask, "Which is uppermost, heads or points?" If the one asked guesses right, she takes one of the pins; if she guesses wrong, she gives a pin.

PUSH PIN.

Two pins are laid upon the table; each one in turn pushes them with her finger; and she who throws one pin across another, is allowed to take one of them. Those who do not succeed must give a pin.

HOUSE-KEEPING.

LITTLE girls are very fond of arranging small furniture in such a manner as they see them arranged by older people. A small table with little mites of cups and saucers, and plates, with little chairs around it, and perhaps dolls in the chairs, is a very pretty sight. In the country, they often take acorns for cups and saucers, and split peach-stones for plates.

NECKLACES.

THE hard red seed-vessels of the rose, strung upon strong thread, make quite a pretty necklace; children likewise string those little round, hollow pieces of sea-weed, which look like beads; and the feelers of a lobster cut into small bits

———

A PARTY.

As children always like to imitate what they see, nothing pleases them more than to play giving a party; bowing and courtesying, and handing round their little plates, &c. &c.

———

SCHOOL-KEEPING.

THIS is likewise a favourite amusement with little children. One acts the part of the school-mistress, and all the others must obey her. They read, say lessons, bring their work to be fitted, are ordered to stand in the corner of the room for whispering, &c. Sometimes they vary this play in the following manner: The school-mistress says, "Ah, Mary, you are a naughty little girl, you tell tales out of school." The one addressed says, "Who told you so, ma'am?" If the school-mistress says, "My thumb told me," Mary must answer, "She knows nothing at all about it;" if she says, "My fore-finger told me," Mary re-

plies, "Do not believe her;" if she says, "My middle finger told
me," Mary says, "Let her prove it;" if the fourth finger, the
answer is, "She is an idle gossip;" if the little finger, the
whole school must exclaim, "Ah, that lying little finger!" If
any one makes a mistake in these replies, the school-mistress
orders some droll punishment, that will make the others laugh.
Care must be taken to order and do every thing with good-
nature and propriety.

———

CAT'S CRADLE.

A PIECE of thread, or small cord, about three quarters of a
yard long, is firmly tied together. Two sit opposite each
other, and by taking it off each other's hands, with different
fingers, and different motions, they change it into a great
number of forms—sometimes a cradle, sometimes a cross, a
diamond, or a spider's web. It is impossible to describe how
this is done; but every little girl will find some friend kind
enough to teach her.

———

INTERY MINTERY.

A COMPANY of children all place the fore-fingers of their
right hands, side by side, upon the knee of the one who is to
begin the game. This one touches each finger by turns,

saying, " Intery, Mintery, Cutery-corn, Apple-seed, and Apple-thorn; Wire, Briar, Limber-lock; five geese in a flock; sit and sing, by a spring, o-u-t and in again." The one whose fingers she happens to touch when she says, " In again," must pay any forfeit the others please to appoint. Sometimes she runs away, and the others have hard work to catch her.

MELON-SEED BIRDS.

WATER-MELON seeds are strung in the form of a diamond for this purpose; that is, first one seed, then a row of two seeds, then a row of three, then a row of four; then a row of three again, of two, and of one. At one end stick a little feather, for a tail, and in the other a morsel of wood for a beak. Leave the string three or four inches long at the mouth, tie the strings together, and pull them up and down; they look very much like two birds fighting.

DOLLS.

THE dressing of dolls is a useful as well as a pleasant employment for little girls. If they are careful about small gowns, caps, and spencers, it will tend to make them ingenious about their own dresses, when they are older. I once knew a little girl who had twelve dolls; some of them were given her; but the greater part she herself made from rags, and her elder sister painted their lips and eyes. She took it into her head that she would dress the dolls in the costumes of different nations. No one assisted; but, by looking in a book called Manners and Customs, she dressed them all with great taste and propriety. There was the Laplander, wrapped up in furs; the African, with jewels in her nose and on her arm; the Indian, tattooed, with her hair tied tight upon the top of her head; the **French** lady, all bows and flounces; and the Turk in spangled robes, with turban and feather. I assure you they were an extremely pretty sight. The best thing of all was that the sewing was done with the most perfect neatness. When little girls are alone, dolls may serve for company. They can be scolded, and advised, and kissed, and taught to read, and sung to sleep—and anything else the fancy of the owner may devise.

FATE LADY.

THIS is a toy made of about a quarter of a yard of paste-board, cut round and covered with white paper. The outside edge should be neatly bound with gilt paper. The flat surface is ruled for mottos, and all the lines meet in the centre. The writer should be careful to draw a line of red or black ink between each, to make them distinct. Exactly in the centre of the circle, a wire is inserted; and on that is fastened a neatly-dressed jointed doll, of the smallest size. In one hand she holds a small straw wand, with which she points to the poetry beneath her. The wire is made steady by fastening it in the centre of a common wafer-box, covered and bound to correspond to the rest of the toy. The doll is just high enough above the pasteboard to turn round freely. When you wish your fortune told, twirl her round rapidly, and when she stops, read what her wand points to.

Here are some verses that may answer for mottos:

"From morn till night, it is your delight
  To chatter and talk without stopping;
There is not a day but you rattle away,
  Like water for ever a-dropping."

"Not all the fine things that young ladies possess
  Should teach them the poor to despise;
In Ellen's good manners and neat little dress
  The truest gentility lies."

"Gifts for Emma and for Rose!
  From sister Sue they come—
How little George will hop and jump,
  To see his pretty drum!"

"Thread, needle, tape, and all are lost;
  Your work-bag on the floor is tost:
Your frock is soiled and tattered too—
  Ah! Fate has nothing good for you."

LINES TO A FATE LADY.

By Mrs. Ann Maria Wells.

HA ! pretty fairy, are you there ?
I know you by that solemn air—
Guiding your mystic wand, with eyes
That feign to read our destinies.
Come—form your circle, and create !
Here's one that wants to know his fate
Nay, wise one, never look demure,—
You're not too modest, I am sure.
Direct thy wand—and let us know
Of brother John, the weal or wo !
The charm begins—his doom is out—
" A wanderer all the world about."

Lucinda's turn—What taste has she
For books ?—or loves she company ?
Ah ! Lady, well may you look sad !
Lucinda's fate is very bad—
" Two dunces her fast friends shall be ;
Herself the dullest of the three."

Maria's fate is more refined—
" 'Tis her's to cultivate the mind :
To be accomplished with good sense,
And meet her talent's recompense."

Come, Lucy, with the downcast eye—
The lady waits your turn to try.
Foolish Fate Lady ! look, what's here ?
Lucy " shall be a—*grenadier !*"

6

Here's little Willy wants to know
The way his future course shall go.
The way to *go?* Ah, Willy dear,—
I'm glad 'tis so,—your fate lies *here.*
The fairy lady seals your doom
In that blest spot—your own kind *home.*

Our manly Tom " shall curl his hair
And be the fairest of the fair;
With rosy cheek, and snowy brow"—
There, strutting Tom! what think you *now!*

Our Anna's pathway lies through flowers—
A long bright lapse of sunny hours;
And while light Bell in sun and play
Trifles her giddy life away,
Sweet Ellen, like the toiling bee,
Shall charm us with her industry.
Fanny in *fishing* shall excel,
And *Peter* live to be a *belle.*

Emma an heiress shall come out,
And shine at ball, and play, and rout;
While timid George, who has a dread
To go unguarded up to bed,
Is doomed—a fate for him how sad!
To march afar, a soldier lad.
A band of warriors, brave as he,
Would form a droll light-*infant*-ry.

But here's Louisa—she must try
The lady's skill in destiny.
Listen!—" A modest, gentle maid;
No foolish airs her mind degrade;
Possess'd of talents, virtue, grace,
Her poorest charm's her pretty face."

I wish the lady would create
For me so beautiful a fate.
But vain the thought; for well I know
That 'tis *within* the power should glow,
To regulate the mind and heart,—
Unaided by her mystic art.
Then, pretty fairy, while you thus
So calmly stand, and point for us,—
I will be Fate Lady—and you
Shall listen to *your* fortune too.

An hour, a day, perhaps a week,
Of you our fates we yet may seek;
Then thrown aside, in some lone spot,
Neglected, you shall be forgot;
Or else,—still worse,—some petted wight
Shall drag you helpless to the light;
And, charmed with your bright painted face,
Shall crush you in his fond embrace;
Thy form no more shall rise elate—
Fate Lady! this shall be thy fate.

INSTRUCTIVE GAMES.

—

GEOGRAPHICAL GAME.

This is played by means of maps pasted upon wood, and then cut into pieces of·all shapes and sizes. In order to unite history with geography, remarkable events are pictured near the place where they occurred. Near Bethlehem, for instance, is a picture of the Wise Men and Infant Saviour; and at San Salvador is a picture of the landing of Columbus. The map is cut into small pieces, and it is the business of the young pupil to put them together correctly.

Sometimes a geographical game is played by means of a board, full of holes, to which little pegs are fitted. On these pegs the names of cities, or kingdoms, are written; it is the business of the player to decide where they shall be placed. The board is marked and numbered with latitude and longitude.

—

There are very numerous games of this kind played with tetotums, and few presents for children are more attractive or useful. There is the map of Natural History, on which various animals are pictured and numbered. The game is played with a tetotum and counter, and the counters are moved according to the number turned up. You describe every animal you visit. The Lion is the point of victory; and there are several laughable rules to prevent your reaching him.

There is a similar game of KINGS OF ENGLAND. The most remarkable events are pictured and numbered; and you give an account of each one on which you put your counter.

The POLITE TOURIST pictures and describes all the most magnificent buildings in Paris.

The PARLOUR TRAVELLER presents to you all the most remarkable places in the world, and gives an account of them.

The game of NATURAL PHILOSOPHY shows you balloons, prisms, steam-boats, &c. numbered and described.

The MIRROR OF TRUTH has pictures of various instances of virtue, accompanied with anecdotes.

There are similar games for JEWISH HISTORY, ARITHMETIC, CHRONOLOGY, &c. all played with a tetotum and counters.

CHINESE PUZZLES.—These consist of pieces of wood in the form of squares, triangles, &c. The object is to arrange them so as to form various mathematical figures.

The preceding plays are quiet and instructive, as well as amusing. They afford excellent recreation for a winter's evening.

GAMES OF MEMORY.

———

I do not introduce these games because I think they will be
of any benefit to the memory; for words without ideas do the
mind no good.   But they are somewhat amusing; and where
a number attempt to say a line, or a verse, in succession, it
affords a good opportunity to collect forfeits.   I have known
little girls who could remember anything you gave them to
learn ; but who in fact knew nothing.   I have seen scholars
who knew every word of their lessons, but did not know what
the words meant.   I remember one, that was asked, " Who
first discovered the shores of the United States?" and answered, "Serpents and alligators of enormous size."   She expected
the question, " What animals infest the shores of the Rio de
la Plata ?" and she did not *think* of the meaning of her lesson.
Another, from the same habit of committing *words* to memory,
without attaching any *ideas*, said that Hartford was a flourish-
ing *comical* town, and Kennebec River navigable for *boots*
as far as Waterville; if he had attended to the sense, he would
have known the words *commercial* and *boats*.   Therefore, it is

only in play that I would have little girls commit a string of words, without caring what they mean. Young ladies should read and study with such habits of carefulness, as to enable them to define every word accurately, whether it be common or uncommon. Now for our games. The House that Jack Built, every body knows: here is one very much like it.

THE OLD WOMAN AND HER KID.

An old woman found sixpence on the ground; with this sixpence she bought a kid; but when she came home from market, the kid would not follow her; she met a dog, and she said, "Pray, dog, bite kid—kid won't go—and I see by moonlight it is now past midnight, and kid and I should have been at home an hour ago." She went a little farther, and she met a stick; "Pray, stick, beat dog—dog won't bite kid— kid won't go—and I see by moonlight," &c. She went a little farther, and she met a fire; "Pray, fire, burn stick—stick won't beat dog—dog won't bite kid—kid won't go—and I see," &c. She went a little farther, and she found some water: "Pray, water, quench fire—fire won't burn stick—stick won't beat dog—dog won't bite kid—kid won't go—and I see," &c. She went a little farther, and she met an ox: "Pray, ox, drink water—water won't quench fire—fire won't burn stick—stick won't beat dog—dog won't bite kid—kid won't go—and I see," &c She went a little farther, and

she met a butcher; "Pray, butcher, kill ox—ox won't drink
water—water won't quench fire—fire won't burn stick—stick
won't beat dog—dog won't bite kid—kid won't go—and I see
by moonlight, it is now past midnight; and kid and I should
have been at home an hour ago."

The butcher began to kill the ox; the ox began to drink
the water; the water began to quench the fire; the fire began
to burn the stick; the stick began to beat the dog; the dog
began to bite the kid; the kid began to go; and the old
woman got home again.

——

THE KING'S GARDEN.

This is very much like the House that Jack Built. One
may try to say it alone, and pay a forfeit for any mistake: or
it may be said by a circle successively. The first passes a
key to the next one, saying, " I sell you the key of the king's
garden;" the next passes it, and says, " I sell you the string,
that ties the key of the king's garden;" the third says, " I sell
you the rat, that gnawed the string, that ties the key of the
king's garden;" the fourth says, "I sell you the cat, that
caught the rat, that gnawed the string, that ties the key of the
king's garden;" the fifth says, "I sell you the dog, that bit
the cat, that caught the rat, that gnawed the string, that ties
the key of the king's garden." My young readers can add as
much to it as they please.

MA VILLE DE ROME.

1. JE vous vend ma ville de Rome; dans cette ville il y a une rue; dans cette rue il y a une maison; dans cette maison il y a une cour; dans cette cour il y a un jardin; dans ce jardin il y a un escalier; sur cet escalier il y a une chambre; dans cette chambre il y a un lit; près de ce lit il y a une table; sur cette table il y a un tapis; sur ce tapis il y a une cage; dans cette cage il y a un oiseau.

2. L'oiseau dit, " Je suis dans la cage; " la cage, " Je suis sur le tapis; " le tapis, " Je suis sur la table; " la table, " Je suis auprès de lit; " le lit dit, " Je suis dans la chambre; " la chambre, " Je suis sur l'escalier; " l'escalier, " Je suis dans le jardin; " le jardin, " Je suis dans la maison; " la maison " Je suis dans la rue." *Voilà ma ville de Rome vendue.*

LE JARDIN DE MA TANTE.

IL vient du jardin de ma tante—O, qu'il est beau le jardin de ma tante! Dans le jardin de ma tante, il y a un arbre— O, qu'il est beau l'arbre du jardin de ma tante! Dans l'arbre du jardin de ma tante il y a un trou—O, qu'il est beau le trou, de l'arbre du jardin de ma tante! Dans le trou, de l'arbre, du jardin de ma tante, il y a un nid—O, qu'il est beau le nid, du trou, de l'arbre, du jardin de ma tante! Dans le nid, du trou,

de l'arbre, du jardin de-ma tante, il y a un oiseau—O, qu'l.
est beau l'oiseau du nid, du trou, de l'arbre, du jardin de ma
tante !

L'oiseau du nid, du trou, de l'arbre du jardin, de ma tante,
porte dans son bec un billet, où ces mots sout écrits. "Je
vous aime." O, qu'ils sont doux ces mots, 'Je vous aime,'
qui sont écrits sur le billet portè dans le bec, de i'oiseau, du
nid, du trou, de l'arbre, du jardin de ma tante !

In the following games it is difficult to *speak* the words, as well as to remember them:

THE TWISTER TWISTING.

When a twister twisting would twist him a twist,
For twisting his twist three twists he will twist;
But if one of his twists untwists from the twist,
The twist untwisting untwists the twist.

———

The same thing in French.

LE CORDIER CORDANT.

Quand un cordier cordant veut accorder sa corde
Pour sa corde accorder trois cordons il accorde ,
Mais si l'un des cordons de la corde dècorde,
Le cordon décordant fait decorder la corde.

———

PETER PIPER.

Peter Piper picked a peck of pickled peppers ;
A peck of pickled peppers Peter Piper picked ;
If Peter Piper picked a peck of pickled peppers,
Where is the peck of pickled peppers Peter Piper picked !

ROBERT ROWLEY.

Robert Rowley rolled a round roll round;
A round roll Robert Rowley rolled round;
Where rolled the round roll Robert Rowley rolled round ?

Similar sentences in French.

IL M'EUT PLUS PLU.

Etant sorti sans parapluie, il m'eût plus plu qu'il plût plus tôt.

TON THÉ.

A Frenchman having taken herb tea for a cough, his neighbour asked him, " Ton Thè, t'a t'il otè ta toux ?"

SI J'ETAIS PETITE POMME.

Si j'etais petite pomme d'api, je me dèpetite-pomme-d'api-erais, comme je pourrais. The second one must repeat this, word for word; and the third must ask, " Et vous, si vous etiez petite pomme d'api, *comment* vous dèpetite-pomme-d'apieriez-vous ? The fourth must repeat this without mistake

DIDON DINA.

Didon dina, dit-on, du dos d'un dodu dindon.

—

SI J'ETAIS PETIT POT DE BEURRE.

" Si j'etais petit pot de beurre, je me depetit-pot-de-beurre-rais comme je pourrais." The next time going round, " Et vous, si vous etiez petit pot de beurre, *comment* vous de petit pot de beurriez vous ?"

—

GROS, GRAS, GRAIN D'ORGE.

" Gros gras grain d'orge, quand te dègrogragrain-d'orgeri-seras-tu ?" Second time going round : " Je me dègrogra-grain-d'orgeriserai, quand tous les autres gros gras grain d'orge se dègrogragrain-d'orgeriseront."

—

The following games have no connection either in sound or sense :

A GAPING, WIDE-MOUTHED, WADDLING FROG.

A GAPING, wide-mouthed, waddling frog ;
Two pudding-ends that would choke a dog,
With a gaping, wide-mouthed. &c.

Three monkeys tied to a clog ;
Two pudding-ends would choke a dog ;
With a gaping, &c.

Four horses stuck in a bog ;
Three monkeys tied to a clog ;
Two pudding-ends would choke a dog ;
With a gaping, &c.

Six beetles against the wall,
Close by an old woman's apple stall ;
Four horses stuck in a bog ;
Three monkeys tied to a clog ;
Two pudding-ends would choke a dog :
With a gaping, &c.

Seven lobsters in a dish,
As fresh as any heart could wish ;
Six beetles against the wall,
Close by an old woman's apple stall ;
Four horses stuck in a bog ;
Three monkeys tied to a clog ;
Two pudding-ends would choke a dog·
With a gaping, &c.

Nine peacocks in the air,
    wonder how they all came there :

I don't know, and I don't care ;
Seven lobsters in a dish,
As fresh as any heart could wish ;
Six beetles against the wall,
Close by an old woman's apple stall :
Four horses stuck in a bog ;
Three monkeys tied to a clog ;
Two pudding-ends would choke a dog ;
With a gaping, &c.

Eleven comets in the sky,
Some low and some high ;
Nine peacocks in the air,
I wonder how they all came there,
I don't know, and I don't care ;
Seven lobsters in a dish,
As fresh as any heart could wish ;
Six beetles against the wall,
Close by an old woman's apple stall ;
Four horses stuck in a bog ;
Three monkeys tied to a clog ;
Two pudding-ends would choke a dog ;
With a gaping, wide-mouthed, waddling frog.

————

Whoever reads this mass of stuff will, I am sure, be of
Harry's opinion, in Miss Edgeworth's " Harry and **Lucy**

Concluded." Do you remember Harry and Lucy's trial of memory? If you don't, I will repeat it for you. " It is much more difficult to learn nonsense than sense," said Harry; "there is something in sense to help one out." "Unless it be droll nonsense," said Lucy; "but when it is droll, the diversion helps me to remember." Harry doubted even this. Their father said he would, if they liked it, try the experiment, by repeating for them some droll nonsense put together by Mr. Foote, a humorous writer, for the purpose of trying the memory of a man, who boasted that he could learn any thing by rote, on once hearing it. " Oh! do let us hear it," cried Lucy, " and try us." " Let us hear it," said Harry; "but I am sure I shall not be able to learn it." "It will be no great loss if you do not," said his father. Harry's power of attention, which he had prepared himself to exert to the utmost, was completely set at defiance, when his father, as fast as he could utter the words, repeated the following nonsense:

" So she went into the garden to cut a cabbage leaf, to make an apple pie; and at the same time a great she-bear, coming up the street, pops its head into the shop. What! no soap? So he died, and she very imprudently married the barber; and there were present the Picninnies, and the Joblillies, and the Garyulies, and the grand Panjandrum himself, with the little round button at top; and they all fell to playing the game of catch as catch can, till the gunpowder ran out at the heels of their boots."

"Gunpowder at the heels of their boots! horrible non-sense!" cried Harry; while Lucy, rolling with laughter, and laughing the more at Harry's indignation, only wished it was not dark that she might see his face. "But can either of you repeat it?" said their mother. Lucy was sure that if it had not been for the grand Panjandrum, she should have been able to say it; but she had seen a Dutch tulip, called the grand Panjandrum, that morning, and she was so surprised at meeting this strange name again, and so diverted by his little round button at top, that she could think of nothing else; besides, laughing hindered her from hearing the names of all the company present at the barber's wedding; but she perfectly well remembered the Picninnies: and she knew *why* she did—because their name was something like *Piccanini;* and this word had been fixed in her head by a droll anecdote she had heard of a negro boy, who, when he was to tell his master that Mr. Gosling had called upon him, and could not recollect his name, said he knew the gentleman was a Mr. *Goose Piccanini.*

"So, Lucy," said her father, "you see that even with yourself, who seem to belong to one of the numerous family of the *goose piccaninies*, there is always some connection of ideas, or sounds, which helps to fix even nonsense in the memory."

"Papa, will you be so very good as to repeat it once more?"

"Now, Harry, let us try!"

"I would rather learn a Greek verb," replied Harry; "there

7

is some sense in that.   Papa, could you repeat one?"   "I could, my son, but I will not now ; let your sister amuse herself with the grand Panjandrum ; and do not be too grand, Harry It is sweet to talk nonsense in season.   Always sense would make Jack a dull boy."

The grand Panjandrum was repeated once more : and this time Harry did his best, and remembered what she went into the garden to cut for an apple pie ; and he mastered the great she-bear, and the no soap ; but for want of knowing *who* died, he never got cleverly to the marriage with the barber.   Lucy, less troubled about the nominative case, went on merrily, "and she very imprudently married the barber ;" but just as she was triumphantly naming the company present, and had got to the Job-lillies, their attention was suddenly interrupted ; and the grand Panjandrum was forgotten.

FORFEITS.

It is extremely difficult to find such forfeits as are neither dangerous, nor unladylike. The following are the best selection I have been able to make:

To laugh in one corner, cry in another, and sing in a third.

To stand in the middle of the room, and first make up a very woful face, then a very merry one; if it be in the evening, a lamp must be held in the hand.

To perform the laughing gamut, without pause or mistake, thus:

```
                    ha
                ha      ha
            ha              ha
        ha                      ha
    ha                              ha
ha                                      ha
    ha                              ha
        ha                      ha
    ha                              ha
ha                                      ha
```

Rub one hand on your forehead, at the same time you strike the other on your heart, without changing the motion of either for an instant.

Two may pay forfeits together in this way: they stand in separate corners of the room; one begins to walk toward the other, with her handkerchief at her eyes, saying in a dismal tone, "The king of Morocco is dead!" The other passing by her, in the same attitude, sobs out, "Sad news! sad news!" Again passing in the same way, they both repeat, "Alas! alas!" This must be done without laughing.

To keep silence, and preserve a sober face, for two or five minutes, whatever is said or done by your companions.

To stand up in a chair, and make whatever motions or grimaces you are ordered, without laughing. Young ladies should be very particular never to exact anything awkward, or improper.

Kiss your shadow in every corner of the room, without laughing.

Repeat, without mistake, any difficult sentence which your companions appoint.

Make two lines of rhyme; or if one line be given, find a rhyme to it.

Say five flattering things to the one who sits next you, without making use of the letter L.

The one who is to pay a forfeit, stands with her face to the wall one behind her makes signs suitable to a kiss, a pinch, and a box on the ear, and asks her whether she chooses the first, the second, or the third; whichever it happens to be, is given to her. The blows and the pinches must not be *too hard*.

Imitate, without laughing, such animals as your companions name.

Say to each person in the room, "You can't say boo to a goose!"

Laugh at the wittiest, bow to the prettiest, and kiss her you love best.

ACTIVE EXERCISES.

SWINGING.

Tнıs game is dangerous, unless used with discretion. Great care should be taken that the ropes are strong and well secured, and the seat fastened firmly. Little girls should never be ambitious to swing higher than any of their companions. It is, at best, a very foolish ambition, and it may lead to dangerous accidents. Any little girl is unpardonable who pushes another violently while she is swinging.

JUMPING ROPE.

This play should likewise be used with caution. It is a healthy exercise, and tends to make the form graceful; but it should be used with moderation. I have known instances of blood vessels burst by young ladies, who, in a silly attempt to jump a certain number of hundred times, have persevered in jumping after their strength was exhausted. There are several ways of jumping a rope:

1. Simply springing and passing the rope under the feet with rapidity.

2. Crossing arms at the moment of throwing the rope.

3. Passing the rope under the feet of two or three, who

jump at once, standing close, and laying hands on each other's shoulders.

4. The rope held by two little girls, one at each end, and thrown over a third, who jumps in the middle.

The more difficult feats should not be attempted, until the simpler ones are perfectly learned. A smooth hard surface should be chosen to jump upon, where there is nothing to entangle or obstruct the feet.

———

CORONELLA.

This is similar to Shuttlecock and Battledoor, but more difficult. Instead of striking the bird with a battledoor, two players throw it and catch it with wooden cups made for the purpose.

[This engraving is copied from a very well written and judicious book, concerning the active exercises of young ladies, called, A Course of Calisthenics for the use of Schools and Families. This book will be useful to mothers, particularly in cities, where it is sometimes difficult to take enough of the right sort of exercise.]

LA GRACE.

This is a new game, common in Germany, but introduced into this country from France. It derives its name from the graceful attitudes which it occasions. Two sticks are held in the hands, across each other, like open scissors: the object is to throw and catch a small hoop upon these sticks. The hoop to be bound with silk, or ribbon, according to fancy. The game is played by two persons. The sticks are held straight, about four inches apart, when trying to catch the hoop; and when the hoop is thrown, they are crossed like a pair of scissors. In this country it is called The Graces, or The Flying Circle.

SHUTTLECOCK AND BATTLEDOOR.

THIS game is too well known to need much description. The shuttlecock, sometimes called the bird, is a little ball stuck full of feathers: the battledoors are covered with parchment; and the object of the players is to keep the bird constantly passing and re-passing in the air, by means of striking it with the battledoors. Some people become so expert at it, that they can keep it up more than a thousand times, without once allowing it to fall. Little girls should not be afraid of being well tired: that will do them good; but *excessive* fatigue should be avoided, especially where it is quite unnecessary.

CUP AND BALL.

HERE a wooden ball, with a hole in it, is used instead of a bird. A stick is made with a cup at one end, and a point at the other. The object is to catch it in the cup, or on the point. The cup and ball are fastened together with a string.

———

SNOW-BALLING.

I LIKE this exercise, because it is played in the open air. Endurance of cold is a very good thing: it makes the constitution hardy. But rudeness and violence must never be allowed in this, or any other game: little girls should never forget that they are miniature ladies.

BOW AND ARROW.

This pastime is common in England, and I wish it might become so here. Of all things in the world, health is the most important. I fear our little girls do not take sufficient exercise in the open air. The attitude in shooting is important. The heels should be a few inches apart : the neck slightly curved, so as to bring the head a very little downward ; the left arm must be held out quite straight to the wrist, which should be bent inward ; the bow is to be held easy in the hand ; and the arrow, when drawn, should be close to the ear. The right hand should begin to draw the string, as the left raises the bow. When the arrow is three parts drawn, take your aim, and keep your eye steadily fixed upon it : the point of the arrow should appear to the right of the mark you aim at ; the arrow is then drawn to a head, and let fly. The trunk of a tree, chalked at certain distances, will answer for a target.

1   2   3

CALISTHENICS.

THIS hard name is given to a gentler sort of gymnastics, suited to girls. The exercises have been very generally introduced into the schools in England, and are getting into favour in this country. Many people think them dangerous, because they confound them with the ruder and more daring gymnastics of boys; but such exercises are selected as are free from danger; and it is believed that they tend to produce vigorous muscles, graceful motion, and symmetry of form.

CIRCULAR MOVEMENT OF THE ARMS.

FIG. 1. In this exercise, one arm, at first hanging by the side, is moved backward; it then passes up by the ear, and is brought down in front. The hand, which is kept folded, thus describes a circle from the shoulder.

This is first to be done with one arm, then with the other, and lastly, with both together—slowly, steadily, and swiftly

POINTING TO THE GROUND.

Fig. 2. The hands are first raised above the head, and then decline forward, the body bending, and the performer points the hands as low towards the ground as possible, but without bending the legs.

THE SPECTRE MARCH.

Fig. 3. The hands are to be placed on the hips, the thumbs turned back, and the performers, raising themselves on their toes, are then to move forward by a rapid succession of very small springs, keeping the whole frame as erect as possible.

THE DANCING STEP.

FIG. 4. The hands should be placed as above. A small **hop** is then to be made on the toes, with one foot, the other stepping forward and repeating the hop; and the performer thus moves forward, by a step and a hop, with each foot alternately.

EXERCISES WITH THE WAND.

The wand for this purpose should be light and smooth, but not of a nature to bend. It is first to be taken hold of near the extremities, by each hand, with the knuckles outward, as shewn in *fig. 5*: then raised to the perpendicular position of *fig.* 6, the right hand being uppermost. The left then takes its place; this should be performed rapidly for some time.

7   8   9

From the position *fig.* 6, the wand is to be raised above the head as shewn in *fig.* 7; it is then to be passed behind, as in *fig.* 8, and finally returned into the first position of the wand, by a reverse progress of the arms, as in *fig.* 9

10   11   12

The wand is to be held as before, except that the knuckles are turned behind: it is then (see *fig.* 10) to be raised parallel with the shoulders, each hand being turned alternately inward, so that the end of the wand passes between the fore arm and the shoulder.

It is then to be lifted above the head, as in *fig.* 11, and brought down behind, as at *fig.* 12. It is finally returned to the position *fig.* 9. These exercises should be repeated many times, till the pupil is very expert and rapid.

8

13

HORIZONTAL BAR.

The performer, taking hold of the horizontal bar, swings backward and forward until the swing is sufficient to admit of taking the hands from the bar, each time of swinging backward from it, and catching it again; but the bar should be relinquished only when in the position described above.

14

THE TRIANGLE.

This is a bar of wood supported at each end by a cord. The two cords meet together at some distance above, and uniting, pass over a pulley, so that it may be fastened at any height to suit the performer. For the following exercises, the bar should be about the height of the knees.

First, for the circle, the bar is held as in *fig.* 14.

The performer then steps round on the toes, gradually increasing in velocity, and bearing more on the bar.

15

STOOPING FORWARD.

The bar hanging in its natural position, the hands are placed upon it, and the body lowered forward, so that the whole weight rests upon the hands and the toes; but one foot may be brought a little forward, as in *fig.* 15.

16

BENDING BACKWARD.

From the preceding position the bar is drawn inwardly, the feet retain their position, and holding firmly by the bar, the body reclines backward to the position shown in *fig.* 16.

DANCING.

MANY people object to dancing, because they consider it a waste of time; but I believe it is only wrong when too much time is given to it, to the neglect of more important duties. Children must have exercise; and dancing is healthy, innocent, and elegant. Those who learn to dance when very

young, acquire an ease of motion that can be gained in no
other way; at a very early age, the joints bend easily; and if
a habit of moving gracefully is then acquired, it is never lost.
Little girls should practise their steps at home every day; it
will serve for excercise and amusement, and tend greatly to
their improvement. Great care should be taken to turn the
feet outward; nothing is more awkward, either in walking or
dancing, than feet that turn inward; by taking a little pains,
the instep will habitually curve outward the moment the foot
is raised from the floor. The arms should never remain
crooked, so as to give the elbows a sharp, inelegant appearance. Care should be taken to carry the shoulders back, and
the head erect; a dancer who stoops, or runs her chin out, is
a pitiful sight. Here I would tell those who are round-shoul-
dered, or carry their heads too much forward, of an excellent
way to cure these bad habits: walk an hour, or more, every
day, with a large heavy book balanced on your head, without
any assistance from your hands. The lower orders of Egyptian women are remarkable for walking majestically and gracefully; and it is because they constantly go down to the Nile,
to bring up heavy burdens of water upon their heads.

Lastly, never toss your feet about, or rise too high from the
floor; truly graceful dancing is gliding, not jumping. But, on
the other hand, you must not walk round languidly and carelessly, as if you had no interest in the dance; what is worthy
of being done at all, is worthy of being done well.

BASKETS.

MOSS BASKETS.

The body of the basket is made of pasteboard, round, or oval, with or without a handle, as you fancy. It should be

neatly lined; and some cover the outside with pale green paper, that any little interstices among the moss may look neatly. The handle should be sewed on the outside, that it may be covered by the moss. A great variety of dry mosses, of different colours, may be put together so as to produce a beautiful effect. Some people prefer to sew them on, because they are so apt to fall off. To be fastened on with thick gum water, glue, or paste. A very pretty imitation of moss baskets may be made of unravelled worsted, of different colours, sowed on thickly, in bunches. Where it is knit on purpose, it must be washed and dried by a gentle heat, in order to keep it curled. Each bunch should

be made of three or four shades and colours, and this should
be mingled in, so as to avoid any striped, or spotted, appearance.   The varieties of green, brown, and light blue are the
appropriate colours : a little black and white may be introduced
with good effect.   I have seen baskets of this kind filled with
the ends of the unravelled worsted, on which reposed a few
chalk eggs, coloured to look like bird's eggs.   I thought them
extremely pretty : but I should not have thought so, had they
been *real* eggs stolen from a poor suffering bird.

ALUM BASKETS.

SUCCESS in these kind of baskets depends somewhat upon
chance ; for the crystals will sometimes form irregularly, even
when the utmost care has been taken.   Dissolve alum in a
little more than twice as much water as will be necessary for
the depth of the basket, handle and all.   Put in as much alum
as the water will dissolve ; when it will take no more, it is
then called a *saturated solution* of alum ; when we say a thing
is *saturated,* we mean that it is *as full as it can be.*   In this
state, it should be poured into a saucepan, or earthen jar,
(by no means put in iron) and slowly boiled until it is nearly
half evaporated.   The baskets should then be suspended
from a little stick, laid across the top of the jar, in such a
manner that both basket and handle will be covered by the

solution. It must be set away in a cool place, where not the slightest motion will disturb the formation of the crystals. The *reason* the basket becomes incrusted is, that hot water will hold more alum in solution than cold water; and as it cools, the alum, which the water will not hold, rests on the basket. The frame may be made in any shape you fancy. It is usually made of small wire, woven in and out, like basket work; but many prefer a common willow basket for a frame; whether it be wire or willow, a rough surface must be produced by winding every part with thread, or worsted. Bright yellow crystals may be produced by boiling gamboge, saffron, or tumeric, in the solution; and purple ones by a similar use of logwood; of course, the colour will be more or less deep, according to the quantity used. Splendid blue crystals may be obtained by preparing the sulphate of copper, commonly call blue vitriol, in the same manner that alum is prepared. Great care must be taken not to drop it upon one's clothes.

In order to have alum crystals very clean and pure, it is well to strain the solution tnrough muslin, before it is boiled.

A group of crystals of different colours form a very pretty ornament for a chimney. They must be made by suspending some rugged substance, such as a peach stone, a half burnt stick, &c. in the boiling solution.

ALLSPICE BASKETS.

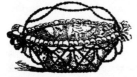

THE allspice berries should be soaked in brandy, to soften them, and then holes should be made through them. They are strung on slender wire, which is twisted into such a form as you please. To be woven in diamonds, or squares, or rows, as you fancy. A gold bead between every two berries, gives a rich appearance to the basket. Around the top, they sometimes twist semicircles of berries, from which are suspended festoons of berries strung on silk, drooping over the outside. Lined or not, and ornamented with ribbons according to fancy.

BEAD BASKETS.

VERY pretty baskets are made in a similar way, of different coloured beads strung upon wire. The wire should be strongly joined; and the place covered thick with sewing silk of the same colour as the beads.

RICE, OR SHELL BASKETS.

THE frame is made of pasteboard, neatly lined; it may be white, or any coloured paper you choose, for a ground-work.

Covered with grains of rice, bugles of different colours, or very small delicate shells, put on with gum, and arranged in such figures as suit your fancy.

WAFER BASKETS.

FRAME make of cardboard, and bound neatly at the edges with gilt paper. Take the smallest wafers you can get; keep a whole one for the ground-work; cut another in halves; wet the edge of one of the halves, and stick it upright through the middle of the whole one; cut the other half into two quarters, wet the two straight sides, and place them on each side of the half wafer; this forms a kind of rosette. When you have enough prepared, wet the bottoms of the whole wafers, and fasten them on the basket in such forms as you please. It looks very pretty to have the whole wafers of one colour, and the rosette of another. If you prefer stars to simple rosettes, you can make them by placing *six* quarters around the half, instead of *two*. The wafers should be exactly of a size, and cut perfectly even. The handle may be decorated in the same manner as the basket; but if it is likely to be handled much it will be better to ornament it with ribbon.

MELON-SEED BASKETS.

MUSK-MELON seed, strung on wire, form very pretty baskets.

FEATHER BASKETS.

TAKE any beautiful coloured feathers you can find, and cut off the quill part. Make the bottom of your basket of card- board; cut it into what shape you choose; at the edges perforate it with little holes; through these holes pass the feathers, having a little of the quill left, and cut perfectly even, so that the basket will stand well. For the top, bend a piece of wire into the same shape as the bottom, but rather larger; then fasten the feathers to it at regular distances. It looks more neatly to have the wire wound with coloured sewing silk. If you fancy it, a wire or pasteboard handle may be made, covered with small feathers. The bottom may be either plain, or lined with gold paper, or have a rice-paper bird, or butterfly, upon it.

CLOVE BASKETS.

THE berry is taken off; the long part of the clove is soaked in brandy, perforated with a needle, and strung on wire, in diamonds, squares, rows, or any other way you can devise. This forms a very fragrant basket.

STRAW BASKETS.

PROCURE a little bundle of straws of the same size; cut them all the length you wish the height of your basket to be;

you must use sharp scissors, and handle them delicately; if the straws are broken, or split, they are useless.

Cardboard must form the top and bottom of the baskets; the bottom must be whole, and the top cut out in a circle little more than half an inch wide; near the edges holes must be made for the reception of the straws. If you wish to have the basket as large at the bottom as at the top, cut your pieces of cardboard of the same size; but if you wish it smaller at bottom, cut them thus:

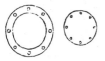

Observe, that when the top is larger than the bottom, there must be just as many holes in one as in the other, and of course they will be farther apart. Remember to have an *even* number of holes, else when you pass your ribbon in and out, two straws will come together. Put your straws through the holes you have prepared, and if you find them rather loose, touch them with gum; leave them about half an inch above the paper at top, and below it at bottom. The edges of the paper may either be bound neatly with gilt paper, or cut in little points, vines, &c. After you have arranged your straw, take quite narrow ribbon, of **any** colour you fancy, and pass it over and under the straws, alternately, like basket-work; ever observing that the straw passed *under* in the first row, must be passed *over* in the second **row**, and so on. Handles of cardboard, made to correspond **with** top and bottom. Bows of ribbon to conceal where the **handle** is fastened. A little painting at the bottom, and a vine **round** the margin and handle, adds to the beauty of the basket.

LAVENDER BASKETS.

In England, they make baskets in the same **way** of stalks of lavender, instead of straw. Those **who** have seen them, say they are prettier, and very **fragrant**.

BASKETS OF MILLINET AND STRAW.

The frame is made of cardboard, cut in such fashion as **you** choose. The easiest kind to make, are where the four sides are nearly square, only each one slanted, so as to make **the** basket smaller at the bottom than at the top; the cover **then** rests upon a square surface. Pieces of millinet should be **cut** just the size of the cardboard; straw must be split even, **in** the same manner they prepare it for braiding bonnets; **the** shreds of straw are then passed in and out through the holes of the millinet, crossways, so as to form into little diamonds. The cardboard and millinet are then fastened together; the sides of the basket joined and neatly bound, with taste; the cover put on with little ribbon hinges. Handles of ribbon. If you like a coloured ground-work, put fancy paper upon your cardboard, before you fasten the millinet on it. This makes a very firm basket. The other kinds I have mentioned are fragile things, intended rather for ornament than use.

PAPER-BALL BASKETS.

THE frame is made of card paper; little rolls of paper about as large as a quill, and as long as your nail, are stuck all about, in the same manner as shells and bugles are put on; these little rolls are made to keep together by means of gum Arabic. When of different coloured paper, and neatly made, they are rather pretty.

PAPER-ROSETTE BASKETS.

THESE are the prettiest of all paper baskets; but I believe it is impossible to describe or paint them in such a way as will enable you to make them; you must see them done in order to understand how they are done. Four strips of paper are cut very even, about the width of very narrow taste; each is doubled nearly in the middle, one half being left half an inch longer than the other; one doubling must be put through the other, and repassed so as to form a perfect little platform of four squares, thus:

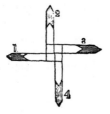

In this engraving the dark parts are intended to show the longest strips of paper, which come down below the others.

No. 1 must be doubled under, even with the square, and come out along side of 3; 2 must pass under, and come out by the side of 4; 4 must pass under, and come out by the side of 2; and 3 must pass under, through the little basket-work square, and come by 1; thus:

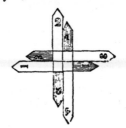

Then take each of the papers, first on one side, and then on the other, and turn them into a point, after the manner of taste trimming; thus:

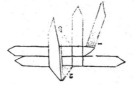

1 is a point just turned backward; 2 is a strip turned back, and brought front again, so that the two edges of the two points meet; and 3 is these two points doubled together, and made into one; each point, when finished, is threaded through the basket-work in the centre. The ends then come in the middle; here they must be again twisted into points, and threaded through the squares; this forms a perfect rosette.

 The ends that hang all around the rosette must not be cut off; they serve to thread through other rosettes, and join them all in a firm web. You can put them on three, or four, or five deep, according to the size of your rosettes, and the height of your baskets.

9

A SHELL BASKET.

CUT a piece of stiff pasteboard, or cardboard, into the shape you wish for your basket; around the bottom sew a strip of cardboard, about half an inch wide, to form a margin for it to stand upon; then cut a round or oval piece, to fit into the bottom exactly, and sew it in; have pieces of fancy paper, whatever colour you choose, cut in the shape of each part of the basket, being careful to have them a little larger than the cardboard pieces, because it is more easy to cut off, than to piece on; make your handle of a narrow, stiff strip, cover it, and line it with fancy paper, and bind the edges with gilt paper; then sew it neatly upon the inside of your basket.   Take as many of those small fluted shells (which come among oysters) as will go twice or three times round your basket; the number of rows must depend upon the depth; make two holes at the small end of each shell, with an awl, as close to the edge as you çan with safety; have *very* narrow lines of gilt paper ready, and gum Arabic, or rye paste with alum in it; fasten a little gilt circle round the outside of each shell, pressing it into the fluted places with a pin.   Then cover the outside of your basket with such paper as you have prepared; after which sew on the shells, close to each other, with strong thread ; when this is done, paste a little diamond of gilt paper over the holes and stitches on each shell; then line the inside of the basket, and bind the upper and lower edges with gilt paper. You must do the things in the order here mentioned, else you will make mistakes; for instance, if the basket is lined *before* the shells are sewed on, the stitches will shew inside. Some cut the upper edge of the basket in scollops, to fit the shape of the shell. The dark lines in the engraving shew where gilt paper is to be put. Make the basket what size you please.

WITCHCRAFT WITH CARDS.

A PACK of cards can be so arranged that you can tell every one in the pack without difficulty, if you have a tolerable memory. First put the clubs by themselves, the hearts by themselves, the spades by themselves, and the diamonds by themselves. Next, conclude in what *order* you will place them. I will suppose that you choose the following : clubs, hearts, spades, diamonds. Then arrange them according to the following sentence : *Sixty-two tens* beat *ninety-three ;* then comes the *king* (represented by an ace) with *eighty-four* thousand men (represented by knaves) and *seventy-five* women (re-

presented by queens). You will begin thus : the *six* of clubs,
the *two* of hearts, the *ten* of spades, the *nine* of diamonds
(you see I observe the *order*) ; the *three* of clubs, the king of
hearts, the *eight* of spades, the *four* of diamonds ; the ace of
clubs, the knave of hearts, the *seven* of spades, the *five* of diamonds, the queen of clubs. Then begin the sentence again,
remembering a *club* was your last card. The *six* of hearts, the
two of spades, &c.

By repeating this sentence after a pack is so arranged, you
can surprise a companion by telling her every one.

ORNAMENTS.

—

IMITATION CHINA.

Choose prettily-shaped tumblers of clear glass; colour an engraving as much like china as you can; place it in a tumbler: cut it to the shape; bind the glass and the paper together at the top with gold paper edging; and put a narrow binding of gilt at the bottom, so as to conceal the glass effectually. The paper will not fit unless it be cut into two pieces; and where these two pieces join at the side, you must put a strip of gold paper on the outside, to conceal it. Some paint a little device on the side opposite the painting; and others prefer putting in delicate coloured paper. You should be careful to get no paste on your paper, before you put it into the tumbler; if you do, it will touch the glass, and dry in spots. No paste is needed at the bottom. A piece of white paper, a little larger than the bottom of the tumbler, cut at the edges, so as to be bent up round the sides, should be put in at the bottom; if you touch the edges of this piece with paste, it must be done very lightly; for if the paste runs down, and gets between the glass and the paper, it will make sad work. When it is finished, not one in a hundred could tell it from French china, without close examination.   A tumbler one size smaller can be placed inside, for water and flowers; but great care must be used in filling it, lest the water run over the edge, and spoil the engraving.

———

STRAW COTTAGE.

Cut a piece of cardboard for the bottom, and make holes at the edges for the straw to pass through, in the same manner as in the straw baskets. For the roof, bend a piece of thick drawing-paper into the proper shape; along each side of it make holes for the straws to pass through; by leaving a wide margin to the roof, it will overhang the sides, and form the eaves. Press some straws flat; and gum them on each side of the roof in rows   For the two ends, called gables, cut a piece of paper to fit into the roof; fasten it among the straws that come up from the side; and ornament it with straw, like the roof. A chimney of coloured pasteboard may be let in, if you like. A good effect may be produced by forming the sides of card-paper, on which are painted doors, windows, &c. like the interior of a cottage; if it be well contrived, the straws will appear like a portico round it. Little temples, summer-houses, and pagodas, may be made after a similar fashion, with round, or six-sided roofs, and an acorn, or some little ornament gummed upon the top. A cottage looks pretty with very, *very* little artificial flowers, introduced among the straws to imitate woodbine.

———

ALUMETS.

THESE ornamental papers are principally for show, although the avowed purpose is to light cigars, lamps, &c. There is a great variety in the manner of making them. Double a strip of paper about an inch wide; cut it across the width into very fine rows; begin to cut at the doubled edge, and leave about the width of your nail uncut at the opposite edge. When wound round and round little rolls of paper, prepared for the purpose, they have a very pretty appearance. Paper cut and wound in the same way, of different widths, makes a pleasing variety: two papers of different colours wound on the same stem, or gold paper and white paper wound together, are very beautiful. Another kind is made by cutting papers about an inch and a half, or two inches long, into the shape of feathers, and then feathering the edges by very fine cuttings; roll them over your fingers, so as to make them curve gracefully; and tie three or four of them upon the stem you have prepared; they will droop over, like feathers in a cap. Another kind is made of very narrow strips of paper, not wider than fine bobbin, wound tight round a knitting needle, so as to make them curl prettily, and then tied in clusters upon a stem.   The stems are rolls of paper about as large as a quill, pasted so as to keep them from unrolling ; they should be nearly as tall again as the vase in which they are placed ; some of the drooping ones should be made shorter, so as to fall carelessly over the sides of the vase.   The Imitation China forms a pretty receptacle for these ornaments.

PAPER SCREENS.

TAKE two sheets of fancy paper, coloured on both sides ; cut them into four halves : and paste them neatly into one long

strip.   Bind one edge neatly with gold paper. Crimp it in fine plaits, smaller than those of a fan ; pass a needleful of sewing silk through the unbound edge, and draw it up close together. Procure an ebony or gilded handle ; gum it firmly on, taking care that it covers the part where the paper is joined ; for the sake of strength, it should go rather beyond the centre. It should be covered on the back part, where it is fastened to the screen, with paper of the same colour, neatly and firmly fastened down on each side of it.   A gilt star, a cameo wafer, or some other pretty ornament, may be gummed upon both sides of the centre.   Narrow ribbon ornaments the handle.

PAPER CUTTINGS.

WHAT is called honey-comb, is made by a very simple and easy process. Double your paper over and over in folds, till you come to the end of it; if you wish to have the interstices of the paper small and delicate, you must do the paper up in narrow folds; if you wish to do coarse work, fold it in large divisions. Remember it is not to be plaited like a shirt-ruffle, or a fan, but folded *over* and *over*. When the paper is ready, cut it slanting, nearly across the width, leaving a little uncut, to hold it together; and turn your paper bottom upward, and cut nearly across the other way; and so on. When it is cut, it looks thus : ⟨\/\/\/\/\/\/⟩ Carefully lay open the folds, and stretch it gently, and it presents a very good resemblance of a honey-comb. Strips of light green paper cut in this way, and hung in festoons about mirrors, pictures, entry-lamps, &c. look very pretty. In England, where they burn coal more than they do here, they fasten sheets of paper together and cut them in this way, to throw over the front of stoves during the summer season.

HEART, DART, AND KEY.

A HEART, an arrow, and a key, may be joined together, so as to have it appear as if they could not be taken apart without tearing them, thus:

The heart is cut into five or six ribs in the centre, thus:

The key is cut as much like a real key as possible, thus:

The arrow is made with a head at each end, thus:

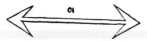

Take one of the ribs cut in the heart; pass it through the handle of the key far enough to admit of slipping one head of the arrow through the rib on the other side of the key; then double the arrow in the middle, and slip the rib back to its place. The handle of the key should be small, and the arrow-head large, so as to make the puzzle greater; for it *seems* as if the arrow must have gone through the key, when in fact it only goes through one of the long-doubled ribs of the heart. If the head of the dart is crumpled any, it should be carefully made smooth.

FOLDED PAPERS.

There are a variety of things made for the amusement of small children, by cutting and folding paper; such as boats, soldiers' hats, birds, chairs, tables, baskets, &c. but they are very difficult to describe; and any little girl who wishes to make them, can learn of some obliging friend in a very few moments. Speaking of them makes me think of a fretful little child, who twisted a paper hat up, and put it in her ear; then recollecting her mother had told her it was very dangerous to put things in her ears, she ran screaming and crying, "Mother! mother! I've got a cocked-up hat in my ear!"

THE THREE CROSSES.

TAKE a piece of paper, half as long again as it is broad.

First, fold it thus: Second, fold it thus:

Third, double it in the mid-   Fourth, double it again in
dle, lengthways, thus: the middle, thus:

When it is double in this manner, cut lengthways directly through the middle, and at one stroke of the scissors you will have three crosses, with the blocks and superscription, which place thus:

CANDLE ORNAMENTS.

THESE ornaments resemble a circle of green leaves. They are made very simply. Double a piece of paper lengthways, and then across, so as to make four thicknesses. Here is an engraving of it:

The dotted lines show the open, or cut, sides of the paper; the others are whole. Cut the leaves as marked in the engraving, observing that the edges come on the uncut side of the paper. When opened, this will be the appearance·

Each of the leaves must then be doubled down through the middle, and crimped fine with a dull penknife, or small pair scissors. If you wish to make them of the bright grass green usually sold, drop seven or eight green kernels of coffee into a cup half full of white of egg, and let it remain all night. In the morning, mix this with melted spermaceti, and dip your papers into it while it is warm. It will produce a brilliant green. Gamboge, used instead of coffee, makes a fine yellow.

LACE WORK CUTTINGS.

THE beauty of these depends much upon the taste and ingenuity of the artist; however, if cut with any tolerable skill, they look very pretty. Do tissue paper up in folds three or four inches wide. In the first place, with pencil and ruler, mark the outside of the fold all over in little diamonds. Then sketch with a pencil any pattern you fancy; perhaps a bunch of grapes at the bottom, and a wreath of roses and leaves running up through the centre. *Between* the figures, cut out all your little diamonds; but be very careful not to cut them

in the figures. This engraving shows the appearances of the paper after it is cut; the dark shades are where the paper is cut out; the white is where it is left whole. Three or four leaves arranged in a circle, cut with some rich pattern, form a very tasteful orna for candlesticks. A hole is made in the centre of the paper for the candle, and the leaves droop gracefully over the side. This work should be done with small sharp scissors. As you cut through all the folds at once, one line of cuttings finishes the whole. The beauty of these ornaments is greatly increased by dipping the paper into melted spermaceti after they are cut. The spermaceti should be melted in a large dish, so that every part of the paper may touch it; the less spermaceti there is used, the better, provided there is enough to touch every part of the paper. Some people obtain glass-dust from the glass-house, and after making it very fine, sprinkle it on while the spermaceti is warm. There is glass-dust of all colours. It looks very brilliant, but is apt to fall off in a warm room. A sheet of tissue paper may be doubled into four, as described in page 141; a bunch of grapes and leaves may be drawn from the doubled corner down toward the open corner, leaving the quarter part of a diamond, at the doubled corner, for space to put the candle in. Be careful to have each grape, tendril, &c. join upon another; else it will fall apart when cut. When opened, four of these rich clusters will hang from the diamond in the centre, in the middle of which a hole should be made for the candle. The clusters should be about a quarter of a yard deep.

IMITATION OF EMBOSSED CARDS.

VERY pretty imitations of this kind may be made in the following manner: Sketch any wreath that suits your fancy around the edge of the card, *lightly* with a pencil. Take a sharp penknife, and holding it edgeways, cut, and very slightly raise up, each line you have drawn with a pencil. If neatly done, it looks very pretty. Some imitate embossed work by pricking a pattern very thick with a needle; doing all the outlines on the right side, and filling up by pricking on the wrong side. A wreath around card-racks for screens, done in this manner, is very beautiful; but it soon gets soiled.

WAFER NECKLACES.

SOME little girls make rosettes of red wafers, as I have described for wafer baskets, and gum them on a piece of red tape, or taste, very thick together, to be suspended round the neck. They look somewhat like coral, but are, of course, extremely brittle.

WAFER ORNAMENTS FOR CANDLES.

CUT a piece of cardboard, as large, or a little larger, than the top of your candlestick; make a hole for the candle, and cover it with fancy paper. On the *edge* of the card-paper fasten a circle of wafers, by wetting them; but before you put them on, it will be well to arrange them in the form of stars, or rosettes, as described above. Flowers can be imitated very prettily by putting wafers, with one third cut off, very thick together, like the petals of a flower. A green wafer, cut in four pieces, and arranged like a calyx, partly resting on the wafer flower, and partly on the cardboard circle, looks very prettily, and makes the whole more strong. Some put in little pieces of bristles, tipped with wax, to imitate the stamens.

ENGRAVED EGG-SHELLS.

Sketch a landscape, or any design you please, upon the shell, with melted tallow, or clear grease of any kind; then let the eggs soak in very strong vinegar, until the acid has corroded those parts not touched with oily matter; when taken out, your drawings will stand out from the shell, in what is called *relief.*

THE LEAD TREE.

Put in a large pint vial about half an ounce of sugar of lead, and fill it to the bottom of the neck with rain water. Then suspend by a bit of silk, fastened also to the cork, a piece of zinc wire, two or three inches long, so that it may

hang as nearly in the centre as possible. Place the vial where
it will not be disturbed, and beautiful branching crystals of
lead will form all around the zinc.

———

THE TIN TREE.

THIS is produced in the same way; only, instead of sugar of
lead, use three drachms of muriate of tin and ten drops of nitric
acid, and let them dissolve well, before you put the zinc wire
in.   The tin tree is more brilliant than the lead.

———

THE SILVER TREE.

PUT four drachms of nitrate of silver into a vial of rain water;
then drop in about an ounce of mercury, and let it remain very
quiet. This is sometimes called the tree of Diana. There
is a close affinity, or attraction, between the metals used in the
above experiments, and the zinc suspended in the solutions;
and that is the reason they separate from the water, and cling
around the wire.

———

IMPRESSIONS OF BUTTERFLIES.

IF you find a dead butterfly, cut off the wings and lay them
upon clean paper, in the form of the insect when flying.

Spread some clean thick gum-water on another piece of paper, and press it on the wings; the little coloured feathery substance will adhere to it; then lay a piece of white paper upon the top of the gummed paper, and rub it gently with your finger, or the smooth handle of a knife. A perfect impression of the wings will thus be taken. The body must be drawn and painted in the space between the wings.

IMPRESSIONS OF LEAVES.

Dip a piece of white paper in sweet oil, and hold it over the lamp, until it is very thoroughly blackened with smoke; place a green leaf upon the black surface, and let it remain pressed upon it for a few moments; then put it between two pieces of white paper, and press it in a book, with something heavy upon the top of it. When taken out, one of the papers will have received a perfect impression of the leaf, with all its little veins. Some think the impression is more distinct, if a little lamp-black and oil be passed lightly over the leaf with a hair pencil, instead of smoking it over a lamp.

LACE LEAVES.

I have tried this experiment without success : but as I find it in a very clever French book, I give it to my young readers, hoping they may have better success than I have had.

SOAK healthy green oak leaves in water, during twenty-four hours ; during this time, draw leaves, birds, or any thing you please, upon cardpaper, cut them out neatly, and pass over them a light sizing of glue, paste, gum Arabic, or white of egg. Then take the leaves out of the water, wipe them, and press them on the cuttings you have just covered with glue. Let them dry together; and then strike upon the green leaf with a hard stiff brush. The leaf being softened by soaking in the water, will soon present nothing but a web of little fibres, resembling lace. The green portion of the leaf remains fastened upon the cardpaper, and when unglued, it is said to look like embroidery.

FLY CAGES.

BRISTLES fastened together with bees-wax in the form of cages, of all patterns, used to be very common in old times. Every where the bristles joined, a scrap of red or black merino, half as big as fourpence, was stuck on. Sometimes grains of sugar, or drops of honey and molasses, were put inside ; but I think this would draw multitudes of flies. These cages looked very pretty suspended from the ceiling.

———

POONAH PAINTING.

This style of painting requires nothing but care and neatness. The outline of whatever you wish to paint is drawn with the point of a needle on transparent paper, and then cut out with sharp scissors. No two parts of the bird, or flower, which touch each other, must be cut on the same piece of paper. Thus on one bit of transparent paper I cut the top and bottom petal of a rose; on another piece I cut the leaves at the two opposite sides, &c. Some care is required in arranging the theorems, so that no two parts touching each other shall be used at the same time. It is a good plan to make a drawing on a piece of white paper, and mark No. 1 upon all the leaves you can cut on the first theorem, without having them meet at any point; No. 2 on all you can cut in the same way on the second theorem, and so on. After all the parts are in readiness, lay your theorem upon your drawing paper, take a stiff brush of bristles, cut like those used in velvet colours, fill it with the colour you want, and put it on as dry as you possibly can, moving the brush round and round in circles, gently, until your leaf is coloured as deep as you wish. Where you wish to shade, rub a brush filled with the dark colour you want, carefully round and round the spot you wish to shade. Petal after petal, leaf after leaf, is done in this way, until the perfect flower is formed. No talent for drawing is necessary in this work; for the figure is traced on transparent paper, and then the colours are rubbed over the holes, in the same manner they paint canvass carpets. In the choice of colours, you must be guided by the pattern you copy. The light colour which forms the ground-work is put on first, and the darker colours shaded on after it is quite dry. Green leaves should be first made bright yellow; then done all over with bright green; then *shaded* with indigo. A very brilliant set of colours in powder have been prepared for this kind of painting; if these be used, they must be very faithfully ground with a bit of glass, or smooth ivory.

If the colours are put on wet, they will look very badly. The transparent paper can be prepared in the following manner: cover a sheet of letter-paper with spirits of turpentine, and let it dry in the air; then varnish one side with copal varnish; when perfectly dry, turn it, and varnish the other side.

SHADOWED LANDSCAPES.

Observe very accurately all the light parts of your picture, and draw or trace them on a sheet of paper; with a knife, or small sharp scissors, cut out all the light places you have marked. It will not seem to have any form or likeness, until you hold it up between a candle and the wall; if well done, the shadow will then look like a soft-coloured picture. A sheet of fine letter-paper placed behind it, and both held up to the light, produces the same, or a better effect.

———

PAPER LANDSCAPES.

OBSERVE well the shadows of the picture you wish to copy, draw their shape as exactly as you can, and cut them out. Paste these pieces on a sheet of paper, in such places as they belong in the landscape: if the shade be rather light, put on only one thickness of paper; if darker, two thicknesses, and three thicknesses, may be used; if the shadow be very deep and heavy, five and six pieces may be pasted on, one above another. When held up to the light, shades are produced, differing in degree according to the thickness of the paper. These make very pretty transparencies for lamps in summer. I have seen china lamp-shades, that appeared perfectly white in the day-time; but the china was thicker in some places than in others; and when the light shone through, it looked like a soft landscape in India-ink.

POMATUM LANDSCAPES.

A PIECE of cardpaper is covered with a thin, smooth coat of pomatum, and then rubbed over with a common lead pencil until it becomes quite dark; not what is called black-lead pencil, but the common lead, called plummet. The *lights* of the picture are then scraped away with a sharp-pointed knife, or needle.

CHINESE BOXES.

HAVE a box of some smooth, polished white wood, such as satin wood, or maple; sketch upon it such figures of cas*'*s, men, women, wreaths of flowers, &c. as you please; then colour all, *except* the figure, dead black. It then looks like ebony inlaid with ivory.

SCRAP BOXES.

THESE boxes, which have been so fashionable of late, are very easily made. The box may be painted white, cream-colour or black, as you fancy either for a ground-work. Then cut from engravings figures of men, women, animals, fruit, vases, &c. and paste them upon your box, arranged in such a manner as best pleases you. When it is covered and perfectly dry, it should be done over with a glazing of dissolved isinglass; and when that is dry, it should receive a coat of copal varnish. The lighter and more airy the figures can be made to look, the better; no heavy masses of ground or trees should be left about them; and if uneven edges are accidentally left, they should be carefully cut.

The paste should be made of rye, with pounded alum boiled in it, to make it more adhesive. The coarsest engravings from newspapers, &c. are sometimes used; but the finer the engravings, the more beautiful the box. Some people prefer coloured engravings; but unless they are very delicate and beautiful, they have a gaudy look.

Scrap boxes are usually glazed with dissolved isinglass, and dried before the varnish is put on; but it is said dissolved pelt is a better glazing. If the box is varnished several times dried thoroughly each time, and finally rubbed with a little linseed oil and very finely pulverized rotten stone, it will look as smooth and polished as a mirror. It is a good plan to do all varnished boxes in this way.

It is common to cover centre-tables and fire-boards with engraved scraps, in the same manner as boxes. When done with great neatness and taste, they form very beautiful articles of furniture. Coloured engravings, if not too gaudy, are more beautiful than plain ones.

Very pretty boxes are made by arranging autumn leaves in garlands or fanciful bouquets. They should be of the most brilliant colours, the hard stems cut off, and the leaves well pressed in heavy books, before they are used. Glue, or isin-glass dissolved in gin, is better for pasting them upon the box than gum Arabic; as the latter is apt to crack, and come off easily. Sea-moss, pressed until it is very flat, and then glued upon boxes, looks very pretty. In both cases, the box, after it is well dried, should be varnished five or six times over, so as to make the surface as smooth as possible.

———

ENGRAVED BOXES.

THE box should be white or light straw-colour, in order to show the faint impression to advantage. It should be varnish-ed five or six times in succession, and suffered to dry tho-roughly each time. While the last coat of varnish is yet so damp that your finger will adhere to it, the engraving must be put on, the right side downward. The engraving must be prepared in the following manner: The white paper must be cut off close to the edges of the engraving; it must be laid upon a clean table, with the picture downward, and moistened all over with a clean wet sponge. It must then be placed be-tween two leaves of blotting paper, to dry it a little. Before putting it on the box, take great care to have it even, and to place it exactly where you wish it to be. Lay one edge of the print, picture downward, upon the damp varnish; hold the other end suspended by the other hand, and wipe successively over the back of the print in such a manner as to drive out all the air, and prevent the formation of blisters. Then touch it all over with a linen cloth, carefully, so as to be sure that every part adheres to the varnish. Leave it until it is thoroughly dry. Then moisten the back of the engraving with a clean sponge, and rub it lightly backward and forward with the fingers, so as to remove the moistened paper in small rolls curled up. When the picture begins to appear, take great care lest you rub through, and take off some of the impression. As soon as you perceive there is a risk of this, leave it to dry. In drying, the engraving will disappear, because it is still covered by a very slight film of paper. You will think it is mere white paper; but give it a coat of varnish, and it will become entirely transparent. Should you by accident have removed any little places in the engraving, touch them with India-ink and gum water, that no white specks may appear; but when you put on your second coat of varnish, you must take care to pass very lightly over the spots you have retouched. The box should be varnished as many as three times after the engraving is on; and suffered to dry thoroughly each time. The white alcoholic varnish is the best. It should be put on in the sunshine, or near a warm stove. After the last coat is thoroughly dry, sift a little pulverized rotten-stone through coarse muslin, and rub it on with linseed oil and a soft rag; after being well rubbed, cleanse the box thoroughly with an old silk handkerchief, or soft linen rag. Some say a very thin sizing of nice glue should be put on the box the first thing before it is varnished at all; others say it is not necessary.

This process requires great patience and care; but the effect is beautiful enough to pay for the trouble.

————

DIRECTIONS TO LAY MEZZOTINTO PRINTS UPON GLASS.

CUT off the margin, and lay the print in a dish of hot water; let it remain on the surface till it sinks. Take it out carefully, and press it between cloths or paper, so that no water may appear on the surface; but the print must be quite damp. Then lay it face uppermost on a table; have ready a plate of pure clean glass, free from spots or scratches; brush it over with some *Venice turpentine*, and hold it to the fire a little to make it run *equal* and *thin;* then let it fall gently on the print. Press it down, that the turpentine may stick to the *print;* also press the print with your fingers from the middle to the edges of the glass, so that no blisters may remain. Now wet the print with a soft cloth, and rub it gently with your finger; the paper will peel off, leaving only the impression upon the glass. When it is dry, wet it over with oil of turpentine, till it is transparent, and set it to dry, when it will be fit for painting. The colours are the usual oils, and there is nothing in the process particular. The back of this painting is generally washed with *plaster of Paris.*

——

I have informed little girls how to do a variety of these things, in which little skill and no practice is required; but I hope they will remember that these things are for amusement only. If they wish to become good painters, they must never indulge themselves in tracing what they have to copy; and they must study well the rules concerning distances and proportions. Sometimes you may wish to copy something that cannot be traced; sometimes it will be necessary to draw objects larger or smaller than your copy—and what can you do then, if you know nothing about proportions? The power of copying correctly from nature is the most desirable of all accomplishments; and in order to do this, you must have a knowledge of perspective, and practise in pencil drawing.

Theorem painting is very pretty; but she who learns nothing else, is no more of an artist, than the one who winds up a musical snuff-box is a musician.

FANS.

VERY beautiful fans may be made with little trouble, in imitation of the ivory fans. Cut the stick of stiff, white cardboard exactly in the shape of those used for ivory. Make a slit about as deep as your nail, in the middle of each stick at the top. Through these slits pass coloured taste, in the same manner you see it done in ivory fans. Glue the taste on the *left* side of the slit in one stick; pass it through the slit in the next stick, fasten it on the *right* side, and cut it off. In this way they will all be joined in pairs; then begin at the other end of your fan, and join these couples all together by the same process. A careful examination of an ivory fan will be of more assistance then the best description in the world. Fasten the bottom with a rivet, like other fans. Paint upon one side, just above or below the ribbon, a wreath of flowers; on the other side a wreath of shells; paint your ribbon in spots, or stripes, on one side, and leave it plain on the other; your fan will then have the remarkable property of showing *four different sides*, according to the manner in which you unfurl it

PUZZLES, RIDDLES, CHARADES.

———

Perhaps some of my little readers will complain that there are not puzzles enough in this book; others will say there are too many; some will complain that they are old, and others that they are too difficult. All I can say is, that I have done the best I could to please them; I have made as many new ones as I have wit to make; and I have preferred old ones that are good, to new ones that were silly. To those who have a contempt for this species of amusement, I will reply in the words of Mrs. Barbauld: "Finding out riddles is the same kind of exercise for the mind, which running, and leaping, and wrestling are to the body. They are of no use in themselves; they are not work, but play; but they prepare the body, and make it alert and active for anything it may be called upon to perform. So does the finding out good riddles give quickness of thought, and a facility for turning about a problem every way, and viewing it in every possible light."

The observing reader will perceive that there are several species of puzzles, distinct from each other, and known by marks peculiar to them. Puzzles and enigmas are general terms, applied to those which come under no particular class A Conundrum is founded on a comparison between two things resembling each other in sound, but not in sense; thus;— Why is a nail driven into timber, like a very old man? Ans. because it is *in firm* (*infirm*). A Riddle describes the various powers and qualities of an object in the most puzzling way possible; thus an andiron is said to stand upon three feet, to run upon none, to bear heavy burdens, to dwell in a warm climate, &c. A riddle can be translated into another language, but charades, anagrams, &c. cannot be. A Charade is made of a word divided into syllables, and each syllable described separately, thus: My first marks time, my second spends it, and my whole tells it. Watch-man.

A Rebus is composed of *initials*, instead of syllables, thus: The first letter of a weight, the beginning of what little girls will be, and the first letter of a musical instrument, make a very unmusical bird. Ounce, woman, lute — O-w-l.

A Logogriph is where the letters of any particular word are used to make other words, by being differently arranged. These is no need of using all the letters each time, and they may be used over and over again; but care must be taken to employ no letter that is not in the original word. Thus in the word *pillory*, may be found *pill, rill, lip, oil, roll, lily*, &c.

An Anagram is somewhat similar to a logogriph; but the letters are not used twice over. A phrase is taken, and the letters must all be used in another phrase made, by transposing the letters—thus in the word potentates, you may find just the same letters that make ten tea-pots. Observe no letter is added, none left out, and none used twice.

A Pun is like a conundrum: indeed, a conundrum is nothing but a pun, put in the form of a question. When a gentleman said of Mr. Hook, "Hook and I are often together," he made a very good pun. (*Hook and eye.*)

Of late, pictured puns have been quite fashionable. Here is a sample.

Fanny.

PUZZLES.

1. **D** What is that boy?

2. **R** What trade is that mill?

3.

stand	take	to	taking.
I	you	throw	my

4. The wicked must 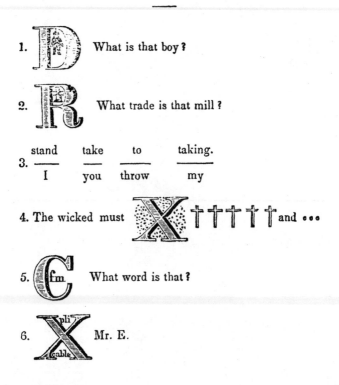 † † † † † and •••

5. **C** fm. What word is that?

6. **X** Mr. E.

7. What word is that?

8. Spell Constantinople, syllable by syllable, without mistake.

9. P R S V R Y P R F C T M N V R K P T H S P R C P T S T N. But one letter is wanting to make a perfect sentence. What is it?

10. Can you draw three rabbits, so that they will have but three ears between them; yet each will appear to have the two that belongs to it?

FRENCH PUZZLES.

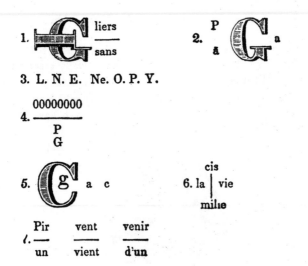

1. G liers / sans

2. P / a G a

3. L. N. E. Ne. O. P. Y.

4. 00000000 / P G

5. Cg a c

6. la | cis vie milie

7. Pir / un   vent / vient   venir / d'un

CONUNDRUMS.

1. Why is the wick of a candle like Athens?
2. Why is Ireland likely to become very rich?
3. To what question can you answer nothing but yes?
4. What kind of fever have those who are extremely anxious to appear in print?
5. Why is a bee-hive like a spectator?
6. Why are fixed stars like pen, ink, and paper?
7. Why is a toll-gatherer like a Jew?
8. What letter used to be distributed at tournaments?
9. Why do you suppose a glass-blower can make the letter E gallop?
10. What class of people bear a name meaning, "I can't improve?"
11. What word asks the question, "Am I strong?"
12. Why was Gen. Washington like an Irishman's quarrel?
13. Why is a greedy boy like a grub-worm?
14. What is smaller than a mite's mouth?
15. Why is a fretful man like a loaf of bread baked too much?
16. Why is heedlessness like a ragged coat?
17. Why should there be a marine law against whispering?
18. Why is a room full of married people empty?
19. What kind of portrait can you spell with three letters?
20. What river in England is what naughty girls do?
21. What step must I take to remove the letter A from the Alphabet?

22. Why is an Irishman turning over in the snow like a watchman?

23. What does a seventy-four weigh before she sets sail?

24. What people can never live long, nor wear great coats?

25. Why are Algiers and Malta opposite?

26. Why is a genteel and agreeable girl like one letter in deep thought; another on its way toward you; another bearing a torch; and another singing psalms?

27. Why is D like a sailor?

28. What is higher and handsomer when the head is off?

29. What word of ten letters can be spelt with five?

30. What word is shorter for having a syllable added?

31. Why is a man who walks over Charlestown bridge like one who says yes?

32. Why is Mr. Bradford's brewery like a Jewish tavern?

33. Why is a theological student like a merchant?

34. If the alphabet were invited out, what time would u, v, w, x, y, and z, go?

35. What is majesty, stripped of its externals?

36. Why is a small musk-melon like a horse?

37. Why is a rheumatic person like a glass window?

38. From what motive does a fisherman blow his horn?

39. What colour are the winds and storms?

40. If a tough beef-steak could speak, what English poet would it name?

41. If a pair of spectacles could speak, what ancient historian would they name?

42. What river in Bavaria answers, " Who is there ?"
43. Why is an uncut leg of bacon like Hamlet in his soliloquy ?
44. Why is a man with wooden legs like one who makes an
    even bargain ?
45. Did you ever see a bun dance on a table ?
46. Name me, and you break me.
47. What three places are like k major, k minor, and k in a
    merry mood ?
48. Why are the fixed stars like wicked old men ?
49. Did you ever see a horse fly through the air ?
50. Why is a Chinese city like a man looking through a key-
    hole ?
51. Why is Liverpool like benevolence ?
52. Did you ever see the elegy on a turkey ?
53. The figures representing my age, are what you ought to
    do in all things.   How old am I ?
54. Why is a very angry man like fifty-nine minutes past 12 ?
55. Why are your teeth like verbs ?
56. Why are deep sighs like long stockings ?
57. Why is a tattler unlike a mirror ?
58. What is placed upon the table, often cut, but never eaten ?
59. What word makes you sick, if you leave out one of the
    letters ?
60. What sea would make a good sleeping-room ?
61. Why would Titian's large daughter, Mary, be like a very
    able statesman ?

62. What belongs to yourself, and is used by every body more than by yourself?

63. Decline ice-cream.

64. Which side of a pitcher is the handle?

65. Where was the first nail struck?

66. Spell elder-blow tea with four letters.

67. Why is a short negro like a white man?

68. Why is a tailor like one who resides in the suburbs of a city?

69. Why is an industrious girl like a very aged woman?

70. Spell the Archipelago in three letters.

71. Why do white sheep furnish more wool than black ones?

72. Why is a Jew in a fever like a diamond ring?

73. Why is grass like a mouse?

74. Why is Mr. Timothy More, since he lost his hair, like one of our southern cities?

75. According to the laws of retaliation, what right have you to pick an artist's pocket?

76. Why is an orderly school-master like the letter C?

77. Describe a cat's clothing botanically.

78. What trade would you recommend to a short man?

79. In what part of London should Quakers live?

80. What difference is there between a live fish and a fish alive?

81. Why is the famous Mr. M'Adam like one of the seven wonders of the world?

82. Why is a miser like a man with short memory?
83. Why is a necklace like a speech on a deck of a vessel?
84. If a farmer asked a barber the difference in their trades, how could he answer in a word of four syllables?
85. Why is a good tavern like a bad one?
86. When is a door not a door?
87. Why is a side-saddle like a four-quart measure?
88. What is that which divides by uniting, and unites by dividing?
89. What is that which is useless, yet a coach cannot go without it?
90. Why is a thief in a garret like an honest man?
91. Which has most legs, a horse, or no horse?
92. If the letter D were never used, why would it be like a dead man?
93. Why is a tooth drawn like a thing forgotten?
94. What is larger for being cut at both ends?
95. Why is A like a honeysuckle?
96. Why is a gooseberry pie like counterfeit money?
97. Why is a man on horseback like difficulties overcome?
98. Why is a beautiful woman in the water like a valuable machine?
99. Why is the letter S like the furnace of a garrison?
100. Why are conundrums like monkeys?
101. Why is Essex County like Chantry's statue of Washington?

CONUNDRUMS OF ALL TRADES.

1. Of what trade is the sun?
2. Of what trade is the sun in the month of May?
3. Of what trade are all the Presidents of the United States?
4. Of what trade is a little tin dog?
5. Of what trade is a minister at a wedding?
6. What trade should keep flies from mirrors?
7. What trade is best fitted to cook a rabbit?
8. What trade never turns to the left?
9. What trade most deserves the gratitude of colleges?
10. Of what trade is the weathercock?
11. What trade is more than full?
12. Of what trade is the manager of a theatre?
13. Of what trade is every child?
14. What trade is very much distinguished in English literature?
15. What trade writes American novels?
16. What trade has been round the world?
17. What trade is most likely to frighten handsome ladies?
18. What trade has not wit enough to keep out of the fire?
19. Of what trade are the greater part of authors?
20. What trade are, all of them, men of letters?
21. What trade is it whose best works are trampled upon the most?
22. Of what trade are all mankind?

THE MISSES.

1. What Miss is that whose company no one wants?
2. What Misses are those whose days are all unlucky?
3. What Miss is always making blunders?
4. What Misses are of very jealous temper?
5. What Miss occasions a great many quarrels?
6. What Miss is a very bad mantau-maker?
7. What Miss is very disobedient and disorderly?
8. What Misses can never find a thing when they want it?
9. What Miss plays more tricks than a monkey?
10. What three Misses are great liars?
11. What Miss is awkward and rude?
12. What two Misses should travellers avoid?
13. What Miss never studied Colburn's Arithmetic?
14. What Miss is very extravagant?
15. What Miss will ruin any man?
16. What Miss should never attempt to translate?
17. What Miss should never repeat anything she reads, or hears?

THE RIDDLING FOREST.

1. What tree takes a gift?
2. What tree is of great use in history?
3. What tree smokes when water is poured on it?

4. For what tree will men scale precipices, and dive to the bottom of the ocean?

5. What tree is a delicate article of dress?

6. What tree withstands the fury of the ocean?

7. What tree is eaten?

8. What tree is an officious gossip?

9. What tree is a city?

10. In what tree would you impound asses?

11. What tree is one thousand pounds sterling

12. What tree is double?

13. With what trees do we speak?

14. What tree do we keep in our barns?

15. What tree would we be sure to lose in a race?

16. Of what tree do we make a wicked manufacture?

17. What tree clothes half the world?

18. What tree plagued the Egyptians?

19. What tree produces more leaves than any other?

20. What tree makes babies sleepy?

21. What bush is superior to all others in age?

22. What bush needs a physician?

23. What bush is not counterfeit?

24. In what tree would you shut up a precious gift?

25. What small tree is a letter of the alphabet?

26. What tree is a lady's name?

27. What bush keeps the floor clean?

28. What shrub is transparent?

29. What tree is an article of winter dress?
30. What is the dandy among trees?
31. What plant makes a sweet walking-stick?
32. What tree is the opposite of all that is beautiful?
33. What tree carries you rapidly to New-York?
34. What tree gives an invitation to wander?
35. What tree is worn for mourning?
36. What tree decorates dresses and cushions?
37. What bush is short and full of trouble?
38. Could this puzzle the trees, and in riddles involve them,
   'Tis the tree I address I call on to solve them.

Moppet.

ENIGMATICAL BIRDS.

1. The bird beloved by Eve.
2. Smooth and quiet.
3. A famous English architect.
4. What wicked men are doing.
5. What we all do at dinner.
6. A plaything.
7. A cheated person.
8. Spoil a metal.
9. What they used to do to scolds.
10. A sound indicative of triumph.
11. Warm country.
12. A tailor's instrument.
13. An instrument to raise weights.
14. What leaves grow on.
15. A bird disliked by mice.

———

ENIGMAS.

1.   A word of four syllables seek till you find,
       That in it are twenty-four letters combined.

2. A young lady had an aunt in prison; she sent her an animal, whose name urged her to escape: and the aunt returned a fruit, the name of which implied, " I cannot escape."

3. The last words of Scott's Marmion are,

> " Charge, Chester, charge! on, Stanley, on!
> Were the last words of Marmion."

The lines occasioned the following enigma

> Were I in noble Stanley's place,
> When Marmion urged him to the chase,
> The word you then might all descry,
> Would bring a tear to every eye.

4. I'm English, I'm Latin, the one and the other:
What's English for one half, is Latin for t'other.

5. I am a man strong and valiant: I have a brother equally
as valiant; but if my brother come to my assistance, I shall
be but half as strong as I was at first.

6. There is a letter in the Dutch alphabet, which named,
makes a lady of the first rank in nobility; walked on, it makes
a lady of the second rank; and reckoned, makes a lady of the
third rank.

FRENCH ENIGMAS AND RIDDLES.

1. Je suis ce que je suis;
Et je ne suis pas ce que je suis;
Si j'etais ce que je suis
Je ne serois pas ce que je suis.

2. Je suis capitaine de vingt-quartre soldats,
Et sans moi Paris seroit pris.

3. What man could have for his epitaph these French notes of music—la, ré, la, sol, la, mi, la ?

4. Mes amis, j'ai vécu cent ans et quelques mois,
   J'amais á célébrer le jour de ma naissance ;
   Devinez de ce jour la singulière absence—
   Il n'est pendant cent ans venu que vingt-cinq fois.

5. Je cause au suppliant une douleur extrème,
   Retournez moi, je suis toujours le même.

6. Je viens sans qu'on y pense ;
   Je meurs à ma naissance ;
   Et celui qui me suit,
   Ne vient jamais sans bruit.

7. Je suis très dur, et je nais dans la terre ;
   Je suis pierre ;
   Renversez moi, je suis un instrument à vent.

FRENCH CONUNDRUMS.

1. Quelles sont les personnes qui ont le plus de caractere ?

2. Quand le ciel est il bon à mettre en cage ?

3. Quel est dans l'histoire le roi, dont le nom offre une demi-douzaine de Cosaques ?

4. Quell différence y a t il entre Alexandre le grand, et une tonnelier ?

5. Quelle est la plante sur laquelle on reste le plus long-temps quand on apprend la botanique ?

6 Quel est de toutes les personages de l'antiquité, le portraite le plus mal fait ?

7. Comment se nomme le septième roi de le dynastie des lapins ?

8. Pourquoi le mouton est il le premier des animaux ?

9. Quelle est la personne qui dort les yeux ouverts ?

10. Quelle est la personne parfaitement sans souci ?

CHARADES.

1. My first is French ; my second is a medal ; my whole is Latin.

2. My first beautiful among beasts and despicable among men ; my second belongs to a family which clothes half the world ; and though my whole is often about people of fashion, it has a stiffness not easily worn off.

3. My first is a preposition ;
   My second is a composition ;
   And my whole is an acquisition.

4. My fourth is to multiply ; my second we ought all to avoid ; my whole the most avaricious will give, and the poorest are seldom willing to receive.

5. My first implies equality ;
   My second inferiority ;
   And my whole superiority.

6. My first is a prop;
   My second is a prop;
   My whole is a prop.
7. My first is sorrow;
   My second came first;
   And my whole come second.

———

FRENCH CHARADES.

1. Le nouvel enrichi porté sur mon premier,
   Qui peut a l'indigent refuser mon dernier,
   Ne vaut pas l'animal qui mange mon entier.
2. Mon tout est grand, fameux en tout pays;
   Otez moi mon second, je suis aux ennemis:
   Otez un pied de plus, ah! ce sera bien pis.
3. Plus d'un auteur, dans mon entier
   A dit des choses inutiles;
   Plus d'un sage dans mon premier,
   Admire la nature et meprise les villes;
   Plus d'un traitre, sur mon dernier,
   Cache par un baiser mille projets hostiles.

———

A REBUS

The sage conducter of a hero's son;
That hero's name, who through great dangers run;

A noble fish, which is by most admired ;
A liquid that by authors is desired ;
A virtue that by all should be acquired.
If these initials are connected right,
They'll bring a charming science to your sight.

RIDDLES. By Mrs. Barbauld.

1. We are spirits all in white,
   On a field as black as night;
   There we dance, and sport and play,
   Changing every changing day :
   Yet with us is wisdom found,
   As we move in mystic round.
   Mortal, wouldst thou know the grains,
   That Ceres heaps on Lybia's plains,
   Or leaves that yellow autumn strews,
   Or the stars that Herschel views.
   Or find how many drops would drain
   The wide-scooped bosom of the main
   Or measure central depths below ?
   Ask of us, and thou shalt know !
   With fairy step, we compass round
   The pyramids' capacious bound,

Or step by step, ambitious climb
The cloud-capp'd mountain's height sublime.
Riches, though we do not use,
'Tis ours to gain and ours to lose;
From Araby the blest, we came;
In every land our tongue's the same:
And if our number you require,
Go count the bright Aonian quire.
Would'st thou cast a spell to find
The track of light, the speed of wind?
Or when the snail with creeping pace,
Shall the swelling globe embrace?
Mortal! ours the powerful spell:
Ask of us, for we can tell.

2. I often murmur, yet I never weep;
I always lie in bed, but never sleep;
My mouth is wide, and larger than my head,
And much disgorges, though it ne'er is fed:
I have no legs or feet, yet swiftly run—
And the more falls I get, move faster on.

———

LOGOGRIPH.

For man's support I came at first from earth,
But man perverts the purpose of my birth;

Beneath his plastic hand new forms I take,
And either sex my services partake;
The flowing lawn in stricter folds I hold,
And bind in chains unseen each swelling fold;
The band beneath the double chin I grace,
And formal plaits that edge the Quaker's face;
By me great Bess, who used her maids to cuff,
Shone in the dignity of full-quilled ruff.
Such is my whole—but parted and disjoined,
New wonders in my varying form you'll find.
What makes the cit look big with conscious worth;
What bursts from pale surprise, or boisterous mirth;
The sweep Rialto forms, or your fair brow—
The fault to youthful valour we allow;
A word by which possession we denote;
A letter high in place and first in note;
What guards the beauty from the scorching ray;
What little master first is taught to say;
Great nature's rival handmaid, sometimes foe;
The most pathetic counter part of "Oh!"
The whiskered pilferer, and his foe demure;
The lamps unbought, which light the houseless poor;
What bore famed heroes through the ranks of war;
What's heard when falls from high the ponderous jar;
What holy Paul did at Gamaliel's feet;
What Bavius writes what school-boys love to eat;

Of eager gamesters what decides the fate ,
The homely rough support of Britain's state ;
What joined to "been" is fatal to a toast ;
What guards the sailor from the shelving coast ,
The stage whence villains make their last harargue ;
What in your head and bones give many a pang ;
What introduced long-tailed similes ;
A preposition that to place agrees ;
A stately animal in forests bred :
A tree that lifts on high its lofty head ;
What best unbinds the weary student's mind ;
A beauteous fish in northern lakes we find ;
A graceful blemish on a soldier's breast,—
All these are in my single name exprest.

———

ANAGRAMS.

Sly ware.	Honor est a Nilo.
No more stars.	Hard case.
Comical trade.	Great helps.
A nice pet.	Lame.
Golden land.	To love ruin.

CHARADES IN ACTION.

I THINK these plays are generally too difficult to be interesting to children; however, I will mention them that they may have an idea what they are.

Suppose the word to be Agamemnon. A little girl comes in dressed like a Turkish Aga, and seats herself on a cushion, or in great fury orders the immediate execution of some culprit she points out. The company are ignorant of the word, but, from the dress and actions, they guess it is Aga. To personify the other half of the word, a little girl comes in and stands upon a chair: she is silent until a light is held near her: then she begins to utter the most musical sounds she can, and when the light is taken away, the sound becomes faint and plaintive. This is to represent the statue of Memnon, which is fabled to have made a cheerful sound when light appeared, and uttered mournful music at its departure.

Nothing then remains to be performed but the whole of the word, which may be illustrated by preparations for the sacrifice of Agamemnon's daughter, Iphigenia, while his face remains buried in a mantle.

ARITHMETICAL PUZZLES.

1. How can you take away one from nineteen, and have twenty remain?

2. What is the difference between twice twenty-five **and** twice five and twenty ?

3. If you can buy a herring and a half for three halfpence how many herrings can you buy for eleven pence ?

4. A and B made a bet concerning which could eat **the** most eggs. A ate ninety-nine; B ate one hundred, and **won.** How many more did B eat than A ?

5. Place four nines together, so as to make exactly **one** hundred.

In the same way, four may be made from three threes, **three** may be made from three twos, &c.

6. If a person hold in his hands a piece of silver and a **piece** of gold, you can ascertain in which hand is the silver, and .n which the gold, by the following simple process. The gold must be named some *even* number, say *eight ;* the silver must be named an *odd* number, say *three.* Then tell the person to multiply the number in his right hand by an even number, **and** that in his left hand by an odd number, and make known **the** amount of the two added together. If the whole sum be **odd,** the gold is in his right hand ; if it be even, the silver is in **the** right hand. For the sake of concealing the artifice **better,** you need not know the amount of the product, but simply **ask** if it can be halved without a remainder; if it can, the sum is, of course, an even one.

7. The figure 9 has one remarkable characteristic, **which** belongs to no other number. Multiply it by any figure **you**

will, the product added together will still be nine. Thus, twice 9 are 18; 8 and 1 are 9. Three times 9 are 27; 7 and 2 are 9. Eight times 9 are 72; 7 and 2 are 9, &c.

If you multiply it by any figures larger than 12, the result will differ only in there being a *plurality* of nines.

8. When first the marriage knot was tied
   Between my wife and me,
   My age exceeded hers as much
   As three times three does three.

   But when the man and wife had been,
   For ten and half ten years,
   Her age approached as near to mine
   As eight is to sixteen.

Ques. How old were they when they married?

9. A room with four corners had a cat in each corner; three cats before each cat, and a cat on every cat's tail. How many cats were there?

10. If you cut thirty yards of cloth into one-yard pieces, and cut one yard every day, how long will it take you?

———

MAGIC ARITHMETIC.

THINK of any *even* number you please, but do not mention it: I then ask you to double it; then I name to you some *even* number to add to it; then I ask you to take away half of the whole amount; then I ask you to take away the number you first *thought* of; although I do not know what that number was, I can invariably tell you the remainder. It will always be just half the number I told you to add. For instance, you think of 8. I ask you to double what you thought of; you know that it will make 16, but I know nothing about it; I ask you to add 4 to it: that makes 20; I ask you to take away half of the whole amount: 10 is then left; lastly, I ask you to take away the sum you first thought of; without knowing what the sum was, I can tell you that 2 remains. This seems very puzzling; but the fact is, half of the sum ordered to be added is *always* left. I requested that 4 might be added: therefore I knew the remainder would be 2.

KEY TO PUZZLES, CONUNDRUMS, &c.

I advise all the little girls not to look at this key until they have tried to guess for themselves at least one hour. Perhaps they will think my putting this caution here, is like the Irishman, who wrote *inside* his letter, "Don't open this till the end of the year;" but if they have turned to the key rather too quick, they can easily turn back, and try again. 'There is nothing like trying;' and even in trifles, it is a good thing to persevere.

PUZZLES.

1. He is independent. (In D, pendant.)
2. It is a milliner. (Mill in R.)
3. I understand you undertake to overthrow my undertaking.
4. The wicked must expect (X pecked) many crosses and little ease (eee's.)
5. Effeminacy. (F M in a C.)
6. Inexplicable mystery.
7. Essex. (S X.)

8. The trick consists entirely in putting out the syllables. When the speller says, " t i," you must shake your head and say, " No!" He will think he has not spelt it right, when in fact you only put out the next syllable.
9. By putting in the letter E, the sentence would stand thus: " Persevere, ye perfect men, ever keep these precepts ten."

FRENCH PUZZLES.

1. G traversé par i sans *sous* liers. J'ai traversé Paris, sans souliers.
2. A long sous P, G grand, a petit. Allons souper, j'ai grand appetit.
3. Helen est née au pays Grec.

4. G sous P sous les o o o rangés. J'ai soupé sous les orangiers.
5. G dans C, a c. J'ai dansé assez.
6. Mille soucis traversa la vie
7. Un soupir vient souvent d'un souvenir

CONUNDRUMS.

1. Because it is in the midst of Greece. (Grease.)
2. Because its capital is always Dublin. (Doubling.)
3. What does Y E S spell?
4. The typhus fever. (Type us.)
5. It is a beholder. (Bee.)
5. They are stationary.
7. He keeps the pass over. (Passover.)
8. Largess. (Large S.)
9. Because he makes a decanter. (D canter)
10. Mendicants. (Mend I can't.)
11. Amiable. (Am I able?)
12. He was a patriot. (Pat riot.)
13. Because he makes the butter fly. (Butterfly.)
14. That which is put into it.
15. He is crusty.
16. It is a bad *habit.*
17. Because he is privateering. (Private earing.)
18. Because there is not a *single* person in it.
19. Effigy. (F I G.)
20. Tees. (Tease.)
21. Behead it. (B head it.)
22. He is patrolling. (Pat rolling.)
23. She weighs anchor.
24. Dwarfs.
25. There is a day in one and night in the other. (Dey and Knight.)
26. *A*-musing, *b*ecoming, *d*elighting, *e*nchanting.
27. It follows sea. (C.)
28. A pillow

29. Expediency. (X P D N C.)
30. Short.
31. He gives a cent. (Assent.)
32. Hebrews drink there. (He brews.)
33. Both study the profits. (Prophets.)
34. They would go after tea. (After T.)
35. A jest. (M-ajest-y.)
36. It makes a mango. (Man go.)
37. He is full of pains. (Panes.)
38. A selfish motive. Sell fish.)
39. The winds rose and the storms blew (Blue.)
40. Chaucer. (Chaw, sir.)
41. Eusebius. (You see by us.)
42. Iser.
43. It is ham let alone. (Hamlet alone.)
44. He has nothing to *boot.*
45. I often see abundance on tables.
46. Silence!
47. Major-ca, Minor-ca, and Ameri-ca.
48. They scintillate. (Sin till late.)
49. I have seen a horse-fly, through the air.
50. It is Pekin.
51. It is founded on Mercy. (Mercy.)
52. L E G.
53. X L. (Excel.)
54. He is ready to strike one.
55. They are regular, irregular, and defective.
56. They are high hose. (Heigh ho's!)
57. One speaks without reflecting, the other reflects without speaking.
58. A pack of cards.
59. Music. (Usic.)

60. Adriatic. (A dry attic.)
61. She would be a great politician. (Polly Titian.)
62. Your name.
63. I scream, thou screamest, he screams.
64. The *out*side.
65. On the head.
66. L O O T.
67. He is not a tall black. (Not at all black.)
68. He leaves it on the *skirts* of the town.
69. Both are notable. (Not able.)
70. E, G, and C. (Ægean Sea.)
71. There are more of them.
72. He is a jewel. (Jew ill.)
73. The cattle eat it. (The cat 'll eat it.)
74. He is Bald Tim More. (Baltimore.)
75. He has pictures. (Picked yours.)
76. He makes lasses into classes.
77. Hirsute, is hairy. (Her suit is hairy.)
78. Grocer. (Grow, sir.)
79. In Hatton Garden. (Hat on.)
80. *A* difference; that is, the difference of *a*.

81. He is the Collossus of roads. (Rhodes.)
82. He is always forgetting. (For getting.)
83. It is a decoration. (Deck oration.)
84. You till, I tie. (Utility.)
85. They are both in-convenient. (Inn.)
86. When it is ajar. (A jar.)
87. Because it holds a gallon. (Gall on.)
88. A pair of scissors.
89. Noise.
90. He is *above*—doing a wrong action.
91. A horse has four legs; no horse has five legs.
92. It would be deceased. (D ceased.)
93. It is out of the head.
94. A ditch.
95. A bee follows it. (B.)
96. It is not currant. (Current.)
97. He is surmounted.
98. She is a diving belle.
99. It makes hot shot.
100. They are far-fetched and troublesome.
101. It has a marble head. (Marblehead.

———

CONUNDRUMS OF ALL TRADES.

1. A tanner.
2. A mason. (May sun.)
3. Cabinet-makers.
4. A tinker. (Tin-cur.)
5. A joiner.
6. A glass-blower.
7. A hair-dresser. (Hare.)
8. Wheelwright.

9. Founders.
10. A turner.
11. Fuller.
12. A stage-driver.
13. A player.
14. A goldsmith.
15. A cooper.

16. A cook.
17. A bell-hanger. (Belle.)
18. A miller.
19. Paper-stainers.
20. Printers.
21. A shoemaker.
22. Dyers.

THE MISSES.

1. Mis-fortune.
2. Mis-chance and Mis-hap.
3. Mis-take.
4. Mis-give and Mis-trust.
5. Mis-understanding.
6. Mis-shape.
7. Mis-rule.
8. Mis-lay and Mis-place.
9. Mis-chief.
10. Mis-represent, Mis-inform, and Mis-report.
11. Mis-behave.
12. Mis-guide and Mis-lead.
13. Mis-reckon
14. Mis-spe.___
15. Mis-managen.e.-
16. Mis-interpret.
17. Mis-quote.

THE RIDDLING FOREST.

1. The palm.
2. The date.
3. Lime-tree.
4. Silver-tree.
5. Lake-tree.
6. Beech. (Beach.)
7. Crab-tree.
8. The medlar.
9. Cork-tree.
10. Aspen. (Ass pen.)
11. Plum.
12. Pear. (Pair.)
13. Tulips. (Two lips.)
14. Cow-tree.
15. The sloe.
16. Tallow-tree. Candles are wick-ed.
17. Cotton.
18. Locust.
19. The paper-tree.
20. Rock-maple.
21. Elder-bush.
22. Fever-bush.
23. Currant. (Current.)
24. Box.
25. Tea.
26. Olive.
27. Broom.
28. Gorse. (Gauze.)
29. Fir. (Fur.)
30. Spruce.
31. Sugar-cane.
32. Plane. (Plain.)
33. Axle-tree.
34. Orange. (O, range!)
35. Cypress. (Cyprus.)
36. Fringe-tree.
37. Life of man.
38. Yew. (I call upon you.)

ENIGMATICAL BIRDS.

1. Bird of Paradise.
2. Halcyon.
3. Wren.
4. Robin. (Robbing.)
5. Swallow.
6. Kite.
7. Gull.
8. Martin.
9. Duck.
10. Crow.
11. Turkey.
12. Goose.
13. Crane.
14. Storks. (Stalks.)
15. Cat-bird.

ENIGMAS.

Alphabet.

Antelope, and Cantelope.

3. If the letter I were put in the place of Stanley, it would make on-i-on.

4. To-ad.

5. Unknown to the author of this book.

6. *Duchess, Marchioness,* and *Countess.*

FRENCH ENIGMAS AND RIDDLES.

1. Je suis un chien ; et je suis mon maître. I am a dog, and follow my master. If I were what I follow, I should not be what I am.

2. The letter A.

3. A man who died of eating two kinds of fishes, called ray and sole, might have for his epitaph, "La ray, la sol, l'a mis là."

4. The twenty-ninth of February.

5. Non, which in French means no : if spelt backward, it is the same word.

6. Lightning.

7. The French word roc, means a rock ; if spelled backward, it makes cor, a hunter's horn.

FRENCH CONUNDRUMS.

1. Ce sont les imprimeurs de livres. The printers of books ; because their types are called characters.

2. Quand il est serein. (Serin.) *Serein* in French means cloudless ; and *serin* means a Canary-bird.

3. C'est Cyrus. In French pronounced six Russes ; which means six Russians.

4. C'est qu' Alexandre le Grand a mis les Perses en pieces ; et qu'un tonnelier met les pieces en perce. The pun is founded on the similarity of sound between Perses and perce ; the first means the Prussians, and the last to stab, to pierce.

5. C'est la *plante* des pieds : the French phrase for *sole* of the feet.

6. C'est celui d'Absalom; parce qu'il est *tiré* par les cheveux. Tiré means drawn and pulled.

7. Lapin VII. (La pincette.) Lapin 7th

sounds in French like la pincette, which means the tongs.

6. Parcequ'il est l'aîné. (Laine.) L'aîné means the eldest; and lainé means covered with wool

9. C'est un doreur. Dort and dore sound alike; one means to sleep, and the other to gild.

10. Un homme sans un sourcil. Souci means care, anxiety; sourcil means an eyebrow.

CHARADES.

1. Lat-in.
2. Buck-ram.
3. For-tune.
4. Ad-vice.
5. Match-less.
6. Unknown to the writer of this book.
7. Wo-man.

FRENCH CHARADES.

1. Char-don. Char is a chariot; don is a gift; Chardon is a thistle, which is eaten by jackasses.
2. Paris. Take away the letter a, and it becomes pris, which means taken; take

away both a and r, and it becomes pis, which means worse.
3. Pré-face. Pré means a meadow; face and preface means the same they do in English.

A REBUS.

1. M-entor.   2. U-lysses.   3. S-almon.   4. I-nk.   5. C-harity.

RIDDLES.

1. The figures 1 2 3 4 5 6 7 8 9, brought from Arabia.
2. A river.

LOGOGRIPH.

The whole is STARCH. The parts are :

Cash, Ha! Arch, Rash, " A, " " Art, Ah! Cat and Rat, Stars, Car, Crash, Sat, " Ace, Tars, 'Has,' Chart, Cart, Aches, Chat, " Hart, Ash, " Scar.

The parts marked thus ["] are words unknown to the author of this book.

ANAGRAMS.

1. Lawyers.
2. Astronomers.
3. Democratical.
4. Patience.

5. Old England.
6. Horatio Nelson.
7. Charades.

8. Telegraphs.
9. Male.
10. Revolution.

ARITHMETICAL PUZZLES.

1. XIX. XX.
2. Twice twenty-five is fifty; twice five, and twenty, is thirty.
3. If a herring and a half are three half-pence, of course each herring is a penny apiece.

4. Those who hear you, will think you say one.
5. 199 9-9.
6. The bride was 15, and the bridegroom 45.
7. Four cats.
8. Twenty-nine days.

AUTOMATA.

Ann. OH, aunt Susan! I have not seen you since you went to Boston. Did you go to see Mr. Maelzel's automatons?

Aunt. Automatons is not a proper word, Ann. When we speak of one image of this kind, we say automaton; when we speak of more than one, we say automata—because the word was originally Greek; and in Greek and Latin the plurals are formed differently from what they are in English.

Ann. I don't think I know very well what automaton means, aunt Susan; but I want to see one very much, because I have heard my cousins tell how very pretty they were.

Aunt. An automaton is an image, which after being wound up, goes by the machinery within it, without any other help.

Ann. Are steam-boats and wind-mills automata?

Aunt. No, my dear; because they are moved by wind and by steam; and the moment the wind, or the steam, is taken away, they stop. A clock is an automaton; because it moves entirely by its own machinery. Mr. Maelzel's images are constructed upon similar principles; and all the wonderful feats are the result of his own knowledge of mechanical powers.

Ann. Do tell me about them.

Aunt. First there was the Chess-player, an image dressed like a Turk : who sat at the board, and played as good a game of chess, as if he had brains in his wooden skull. He shook his head, and rapped the board with his fingers, when his adversary made a move contrary to the rules of the game ; and when he had the king in his power, he called " Echec ! " which is the French word for " Check ! "

Then there was a large Trumpeter dressed in scarlet uniform, whose music was enough to make one's heart leap. The children were particularly delighted with the little figures n the carousel.

Ann. What is the meaning of *carousel ?*

Aunt. It is the name of a military game in France. The scenery represents a circus, with a fountain in the centre ; and a number of little figures ride round the circus, performing feats to excite the wonder of the spectators.

One called the Spanish Lancer, catches a little cap on the point of his lance, without stopping his horse, and rides off with it in triumph. Here is a picture of him.

Ann. He looks like a real boy; but I think the horse looks clumsy.

Aunt. That is because he is a wooden horse, with jointed legs. You cannot expect him to canter quite as well as a rea' horse. Here is another of the figures, called the Marksman ol

Madrid. With a pistol no bigger than your thumb, he aimed at a little bird, on a post. The pistol went off with real fire and smoke, and the bird fell down dead.

Another was a famous Vaulter. He jumped over standards,

placed at a height, which might be called *immense* when com-

pared with him and his horse; yet he was always sure to
alight safely on his saddle.

A slow, awkward Clown was pursued by a hungry Horse,
who at last overtook him and snatched his cap from his head.
Here is a picture of the Horse and Clown.

His friend Harlequin came to his rescue; but Harlequin's
horse behaved very ill. He kicked, and plunged, and reared,
and finally threw his poor rider off entirely. This made the
little children laugh greatly. Here is a picture of the Harlequin.

The little girl who danced the Wreath-dance on horse-back, was as graceful as any of them. I cannot tell you half the feats these automata performed. If ever Mr. Maelzel comes to Boston again, I will send for you, and take you to see them. Here is a picture of the little Wreath-dancer.

Ann. Dear aunt, do tell me about those cunning little poppets, the Rope-Dancers.

Aunt. To me, they were the most wonderful of the whole. These two little figures performed all manner of feats on a rope suspended across the room. Sometimes they were seated firmly, with arms outstretched : sometimes they turned heels over head ; sometimes they hung with head downward, and sometimes they were suspended only by one foot. This was all done so naturally, that it really seemed as if the little creatures were alive. I felt half afraid they would tumble and break their bones. By moving the limbs of these figures, they could be made to utter quite distinctly, "Mamma!" "Papa!" and "La! la!" Here is a picture of one of them.

Ann. This is so very wonderful, that I should not believe it, if you did not tell me you had seen it. Is Mr. Maelzel the only man who can make such strange things?

Aunt. No, my dear; very extraordinary things of this kind have been made in different parts of the world. There is a mechanic in Geneva, Switzerland, who is famous among all the civilized nations of the earth. He made the little jewelled mice, exhibited in London a few years ago.

These mice would pick up the crumbs from the floor, and prick up their ears and scamper, when they heard a noise, just like living mice. Even the cat was so much deceived, that she actually caught one of them.

The same man likewise made very perfect caterpillars. They would crawl along, and you could see all the soft down on them move as they went; when touched with a pin, they would coil themselves up, as if they were in pain. This was all effected by machinery inside their bodies ; they were wound up, just like watches.

Ann. Did you see any of this man's works ?

Aunt. I once saw a very beautiful musical snuff-box made by him. When a spring was touched, a little bird would rise up, and sing, or seem to sing, the sweetest tunes. He was not longer than my thimble ; yet he was so perfect, little feathers and all, that I almost imagined he was alive. He pecked under his wings, looked up sideways, and closed his eyes, just as a real bird would do. I have heard of another musical box, by the same mechanic, where a whole cage full of birds sung together. I am such a dear lover of freedom, that birds in a cage would never *seem* to me to sing half so merrily, as those perched on a tree—even if I knew they were automata.

The little Duke of Bordeaux, grandson of the late King of France, had an automaton goose presented him, which was so perfect in all respects, that those who saw it could not be convinced it was a machine, until they had handled it. It would even swallow the corn that was thrown to it.

Ann. I don't think it was a great compliment to his little highness, to give him a goose. I think I should have liked the jewelled mice better.

Aunt. Should you have liked the famous automaton lady, as large as life, who played upon the piano, moved the pedal with her feet, rolled her eyes, and who even seemed to breathe ?

Ann. No, indeed, I should not. I think it would make me

something like afraid, to see anything so very much like life, and yet not alive. Are you going away? Do tell me some more.

Aunt. Ever since you could speak, you have teased me for stories. The moment I finished one, you used to say, "more again, aunt Susan!" But indeed I am too much engaged to tell you "more again," at present. I wish you to go and hunt up your old doll, that you may dress it for your little sister Jane. When that is done, I will come back and show you how to finish the pretty little needle-book you began yesterday.

FAREWELL TO MY DOLL.

BY MRS. ANN MARIA WELLS.

My old acquaintance! many a year
Has gone since last I met you here;
And many a change has taken place,
Since last I saw that smiling face.
But you—except a change of clothes,
And just a tip gone from your nose—
Are still smooth-browed, red-cheeked, and calm,
As last you lay upon my arm.
Those bright orbs stare, those ringlets flow,
Just as they did five years ago;
When with a sad, reluctant heart,
I fixed the day that we should part;

And promised, all for learning's sake,
Our sweet companionship to break.
I, with my flowing tears the while,
You, with that same unchanging smile:
Indeed, I thought it very hard
So little of my grief you shared.
To you I always turn'd, whene'er
My little bosom felt a care;
To you I told the piteous tale,
And comfort never seem'd to fail.
Shall I again, whate'er my want,
E'er find so *safe* a confidant?

But past the time for childish toys—
I feel that there are higher joys;
And things once dim and undefined,
Now shed clear light upon my mind
I've learn'd to listen to the voice
Of conscience; and my heart makes choice
Of precious things, that teach me true,
Where praise, and prayer, and love are due
The skies, the hills, the shady nooks,
And those sweet hoards of pleasure—books
These have I learn'd to love; for they
Bring some new blessing every day.

NEEDLE-WORK.

PLAIN SEWING.

THERE is no accomplishment of any kind more desirable for a woman, than neatness and skill in the use of a needle. To some, it is an employment not only useful, but absolutely necessary; and it furnishes a tasteful amusement to all. The first and most important branch, is plain sewing. Every little girl, before she is twelve years old, should know how to cut and make a shirt with perfect accuracy and neatness. Awkwardness and want of judgment are shown in small things, as well as in great. I have seen young ladies make sleeves and sew them into the shirt, before the wristbands were put on; and every other part finished, before the linings were placed on the shoulder; and when I have spoken of it, I have heard them exclaim, "La! what matter is it which is done first?" I never have a high opinion of little girls, who frequently say, "I don't care," or "what matter is it?" The fact is, it is a great deal of consequence what parts of a shirt are first finished; by a little judgment. much time and in-

convenience may be saved. The sleeves should first be hemmed on each side, about a finger's length, then neatly gathered with strong thread, waxed with white wax; (some use
white silk, instead of thread, but it is apt to grow yellow by
washing;) two threads should be taken up by the needle, and
four left; .if in any instance the needle is placed above or below the original thread, so as to make the gathering look
uneven, the work should immediately be undone; each gather
must be made smooth, both above and below the gathering-
thread, by means of a small pointed pin; the wristband should
be sewed on before the sleeve is made, for the simple reason
that it is very inconvenient to do it afterward. The linings
for the shoulder should be basted on, before the sides of the
shirt are sewed; and the sleeves put in before the collar is
on—for the same reason.

In stitching, no more than two threads should be taken,
either back of the needle, or before it, however fine the texture of the cloth. Care should be taken not to leave a thread,
as it spoils the beauty of the work.

Button-holes should be neatly overcast, about three or four
threads deep; never deeper than is necessary for strength, for
broad work of this kind always appears clumsy; little bars
should be formed across the corners and neatly worked, just
the depth of the sides; in working button-holes, the thread
should always be thrown *forward* before catching up the loop
on the needle; this makes a wonderful difference in the beauty
of the edge.

The width between the edge of the collar and wristbands, and the thread drawn for stitching, is entirely a matter of taste. It is the fashion to leave a wide space; and it is certainly the best economy—as when the edge is worn out, it can be cut off, and sewed neatly. The width between the stitching and the edge should correspond exactly in every part of the shirt.

What are called hem-fells, are more neat than any other: the raw edge is first turned down very even; and then turned back, like a hem wrong side outward, before the sides are sewed together. The corners of hems should be very neatly managed—no knots tied, no little shreds left out; and the bottom edge should not be turned over the side at one end, and the side edge turned over the bottom, at the other end: to avoid this, the sides should both be hemmed before the bottom.

The neck-gussets are usually stitched in the same manner as the wristband, and sewed into the shoulder, over and over; but it is stronger and looks more neatly, to leave the gusset with edge unturned, and stitch the shirt upon it, in two rows of stitching, as deep as the wristband; only one thread should be left between the stitching and the gusset, where the shirt joins upon it. The inside half of the neck-gusset should be sewed to the shoulder lining, over and over, on the wrong side, and fitted exactly to the outside half. When the neck is gathered for the collar, the inside and outside half of the gusset ought to be gathered separately.

The side-gussets look better, and are stronger, for being stitched across. The usual length left open for the arm-holes, sides, and bosom, is a quarter of a yard and a nail; the bosom sets better for being sloped a very little before it is set into the collar. The collar is usually a little short of half a yard long, and half a quarter and a nail wide, when doubled. The wrist-bands are a quarter of a yard long, and half a quarter wide, when doubled; some prefer them rounded at the corners, as being less troublesome about writing, &c. The space into which the sleeve is gathered at the arm-hole, should exactly correspond to the length of the wristband. Some make the length of the shoulder half a quarter, and others, half a quarter and a nail. Different people have very different rules; it is therefore proper for little girls to cut and measure a shirt, by some pattern that is given them.

At the infant schools in England, children of three and four years old make miniature shirts, about big enough for a large doll. At first, they learn to turn a hem on paper very even; then they turn a fell; when quite perfect in this, they are allowed to do the same things with cloth; then they hem with bright-coloured silk, so that every stitch may be seen distinctly; then they sew over and over, in the same way; then they stitch and gather, &c. I have seen a small fine linen shirt made with crimson silk, by an English child of five years old and it was truly beautiful.

Those little girls who wish to keep a neat work-box, will

do well to take care of their tape in the following manner. Take a piece of pretty silk cord, or very narrow taste, about three or four inches long; wind your tape around this, and when it is all wound, tie the cord so as to confine the end. You will never need to undo this knot; you have only to take hold of the end of the tape and press backward against the cord, a little, when you want to unwind the tape; and if you take off too much, you have merely to slip the cord along until it is wound up again. This picture shows how it looks with a little piece unwound.

MENDING.

Stockings should be mended on the wrong side; the stitches very near each other; small loops left, when the needle is drawn through, because the yarn will shrink in washing; in weaving across, take up but one thread and leave but one, changing the threads each time you go across. Little girls can mend as neatly as women, if they will have patience; the only difficulty is, they are in such a hurry, that they take up two threads at once, or leave the same threads the second time across, that they did at first.

Patches should always be well shaped, and basted on perfectly even; a round, angular, or slanting patch, is the sure
sign of a slut.

Where there are stripes, checks or figures, in the garment
to be mended, they should be matched as nearly as possible,
that the patch may not be seen. Those who are patient in
trifles, are likely to do great things well. "*Petit a petit, l'oiseau fait son nid.*"

———

BAGS.

OF these there is too great a variety to mention. Silk, with
covered cord sewed in between the seams; scalloped, or pointed at the top; lined with some bright colour; covered cord
stitched all around the scallops; and the strings run in about a
finger's depth from the top, forms a very pretty and genteel bag.

———

RIBBON BAGS.

RIBBON sewed together, left open two or three inches at the

top, and turned down thus,   so as to form points

above the strings, is very pretty. A much prettier bag is fa-
shioned of ribbon thus: take a yard and a half, or two yards. of
ribbon; gather it in the centre; stitch the outside edges to-

gether, except three or four inches left open and lined for strings. A small ornamental button should be placed in the centre. Here is an outline of it:

BALLOON BAGS.

WHAT is called a balloon bag, is made of pasteboard covered with silk, and the edges bound neatly with narrow taste before they are sewed together. It may be made of three, or four, or five pieces, just as you fancy. In one place, the edges are not sewed together, in order to leave an opening for the ball of thread. Some are made large, and some very small. This is the shape of the pieces:

BEAD BAGS.

BEAD Bags are so much work, that it is seldom worth while to make them. They are done on canvass, similar to that used for marking. The flowers or other ornaments you intend to work are drawn; and strings of beads are then sewed on, of

14

such colours and shades as your fancy, or your pattern may dictate. The spaces between your fingers must all be filled up with beads of the same colour, to form a ground. The toilsome process of stringing beads may be avoided in the following manner : when purchased, they are strung on grass, and tied together in bunches ; untie them carefully, wax your silk, pass the end of it between your nails till you get it worn down fine and soft ; then wax it, and twist it round the end of the grass firmly, then let the beads slip down from the grass to the silk : if care is taken, a whole string can thus be transferred in a minute. When you wish to split sewing silk, always wax it before you try to separate it.

BEAD WORK.

A GREAT variety of beautiful work may be done with beads, besides bags and purses. Necklaces strung in chains, or festoons, or diamonds, or so as to form a hollow tube, furnish an amusing employment for little girls. They should be strung on horse-hair, or a species of strong white grass, sold for that purpose. Little shoulder-bracelets for infants' sleeves are easily made, and are very pretty. Red, or blue, or white beads strung in diamonds, with a gold bead at every corner of the diamond, are quite tasteful. Some form imitation of flowers, by using beads of different shades and colours, after the same fashion as flowers are marked on a sampler: in this case, the beads must be sewed upon a narrow bit of linen, and all the spaces between the flowers be filled with one colour, and the linen afterward lined with that narrow kind of ribbon called taste. In all cases, shoulder-bracelets should have an inch or two of taste at each end, to tie them with; it should be of the same colour as the beads.

THREAD BAG.

A VERY neat little bag for balls of cotton is made thus : two thicknesses of silk are joined together by runnings, about an inch, or more, apart, and cotton is passed through the runnings, in the same manner as the little quilted bonnets; at the top, both pieces of silk are hemmed and left open, between the runnings; at the bottom, both are gathered round in a small circular piece of pasteboard; another piece of pasteboard of the same size, with a narrow piece of ribbon, or taste, between them, forms a convenient little pin-ball. Some add a couple of flannel leaves, and another circular piece of pasteboard, neatly covered with silk; and thus form a needle-book and pincushion together.

I forgot to mention, that the lining of the bag must be hemmed, and left open *below* the strings. Five or six balls of cotton may be kept in the open spaces between the runnings, without any danger of becoming dirty, or entangled.

RIBBON BAG, OR BOX.

Two sides and two ends must first be cut in cardboard and these must be covered with narrow ribbon, about an inch wide. The ends must be about an inch and a half long, and the sides must be about twice as long. They must be neatly lined with silk or ribbon. Two sides must then be fitted, each just as wide as the length of the ends, and just as long as the length of the side pieces. These are neatly covered and lined; on the outside of each, a little ribbon bag is gathered, which is hemmed at the top, and tied with a bit of taste. The inside of one is stuffed, between the card and the lining, so as to answer for a pincushion. On the other side, two or three leaves are placed for a needle-book, and loops made for a bodkin. All the edges are bound neatly; all sewed together at the bottom, but left open at the sides and top. At the top, a little loop is sewed upon each corner. A string is fastened at one corner, and passed through the loop at the other corner; another string is fastened at the opposite corner, and passed through the other loop; these two strings are then tied together. When all this is done, one end is fixed; the other end is to be done in the same way; and then the bag can be easily drawn open and closed, by means of the strings.

PINCUSHIONS.

THE forms into which pincushions have been manufactured of late, are almost without number. The most common kind consists of two circles of pasteboard, covered with silk, with narrow ribbon sewed between, and stuffed with bits of flannel cut of the size of the pasteboard. Cotton is very bad for the stuffing, because the pins enter it with difficulty; and when the cushions are of such a shape that they can be stuffed with flannel, it is much preferable to wool. When sewed with silk of a very decided colour, and the stitches taken with great regularity, an edge resembling delicate cord may be produced.

Some cut the pasteboard into oblong pieces, and then paint rabbits, or squirrels, of a size suitable to cover each side, and after the cushion is made, they paste them on; the places for the pins then come between the two rabbits. Others paint a cat seated, for each side, and make the cushion of such a shape as will fit in well. Some cut the figures of the cats in black velvet, and put little spangles for eyes. I have seen butterflies painted and pasted on each side, in the same way. Some do the paintings on rice paper, and put them on cardboard, cut out precisely in the shape of the figure. They look richer, but are more easily injured. A very pretty pincushion may be made in the shape of a small easy-chair.

There is an old-fashioned kind of pincushion which looks rather clumsy, but it is extremely convenient for a journey.

The cushion is nearly an inch thick; no pasteboard is put on the outside, in order that there may be more room for pins; the inside is a piece of cardboard, covered with silk; a round hole is cut in it, and a piece of cardboard, just big enough for a thimble, let in. Little bars, stitched across on each side of the thimble hole, form places for scissors and bodkin. All this should be arranged before the stuffing is put in, and the bit of silk on the outside fitted; it is very inconvenient doing it afterward. The pincushion forms but half of the establishment. Flannel leaves are put in for needles, and the outside is of covered silk, with a little pocket for thread. This pocket consists of a plain piece of silk, nearly the size of the pasteboard, fastened to the outside by means of little gores at each end.

What used to be made in old times, and called housewives, were similar to the travelling pincushion. These had a piece of silk, the same width as the cushion, and little more than a quarter of a yard long, neatly stitched into compartments, to answer the purpose of thread papers. This was rolled round the cushion, and fastened by a small loop and button. Housewives were very useful things, but they are out of fashion now.

Pincushions cut in the shape of a harp, or guitar, with taste between the two sides, are very pretty. Gold thread can be used to imitate the strings of the instrument. Very handsome pincushions for the toilet are made of well-dressed dolls, stuffed from the waist to the feet, so as to produce the appearance of a fashionable gown. Another toilet cushion is very pretty and convenient, made of bits of ribbon, so as to form a six-sided circle. This is the shape of each piece:

When put together, this is the appearance of it ·

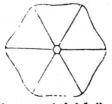

The little hole in the centre is left hollow. The pearl edges of the ribbon are stitched together at the outside. The edge is left perfectly straight; the pretty scalloped appearance is merely a little jutted out, where the slanting edges of the six bits of ribbon are sewed together. The beauty of the shape depends a good deal upon its being stuffed full, plump, and even.

What are called "bachelor's pincushions," are made very thin, so that gentlemen can carry them in their pockets with convenience. No margin of ribbon, or taste, is put between the bits of pasteboard, in making these cushions. Two round pieces of pasteboard are covered with silk, and neatly sewed together, with one or two thin pieces of flannel between them. Of course, merely one circle of pins can be put in.

Very pretty ones are made in the shape of bellows. A hole is left, to put in a tape-needle, which represents the nose. The military hat, called *chapeau de bras*, is a very pretty form for these kind of cushions. The piece let in at the top between the pasteboard, should be wide in the middle, and taper off to nothing at the ends. It should likewise be stuffed, so as to look bigger at top than bottom, like a chapeau partly open. A little cockade at the side, and gold tassels at the ends, make it look finished tastefully. Butterfly pincushions, well made, are extremely beautiful. There are four wings, each made of two bits of covered cardboard, sewed together, without stuffing. On the outside, the wings are painted as nearly like a butterfly as possible. The body is made of black velvet, with wings of yellow silk, or gold thread; if filled with emery, it answers a very good purpose. The only place for pins is around the edges of the wings.

Another pincushion, prettier than any I have seen, is made in imitation of a fish. The cardboard is covered with silk, painted as naturally as possible; and the two sides are sewed together, with very little stuffing in the middle, and none at the tail. The pins are so arranged as to represent the fins. The dolphin and the trout are prettier to imitate, than any other fish.

EMERY-BAGS.

EMERY-BAGS are made in various forms. Some are merely little square bags, stuffed hard with emery; others are made round, and painted like an apple, plum, or peach; others imitate a little barrel, with cord put round for hoops. But the prettiest are imitations of strawberries, made of crimson merino, worked with green and brown silk to represent the calyx and spots of the strawberry. Unless these bags are made of very firm stuff, they should be lined; for the emery is exceedingly apt to sift out.

NEEDLE-BOOKS.

NEEDLE-BOOKS are usually made with a pincushion on one side; that is, instead of two thin covers merely, one side consists of two pieces of pasteboard, with a margin of ribbon between, and stuffed with flannel. The flannel leaves for needles should be of different sizes, neatly cut in delicate points around the edge, or worked with coloured silk. These books can be round or square, or oblong, according to fancy. Some make butterfly needle-books; the outside wings of embroidered velvet; the inside of silk; and flannel, for needles, between. The body is stuffed with emery.

There is a kind of needle-book called the fish's mouth. It consists of two covered bits of pasteboard, sewed together neatly at the sides, left wholly open at the top, and partly open at the bottom. The flannel leaves are fastened upon a long bit of ribbon, which is put through the hole at the bottom, and then tied in a knot, to prevent its slipping out. By taking hold of the ribbon at top, you can pull the leaves out; and by taking hold at the bottom, you can draw them back again. Here is a picture of it:

PURSES.

Bead purses may be made in the same way as bead bags; but they are hardly worth the time and trouble. Very handsome purses may easily be made of silk cord. Arrange the cord on your fingers according to the size you wish the purse to be at top, and fasten it; still keeping the cord on your fingers, pass round the second row under the first. Take sewing silk, of some colo r that will form a pretty contrast to the cord, and at regular distances fasten the two rows of cord together, by passing the sewing silk through twice, in imitation of button-hole stitch. The next time going round, fasten in the same way; but instead of making one fastening directly under the other, make it in the middle of the space you left the last time: this forms a diamond. The silk is passed along on the inside, between the fastenings. The size of the diamonds, of course, depends on the length of the spaces left. When you think the purse is long enough to be narrowed, draw the cord into smaller and smaller circles, till you come to a point.

———

Little girls often work purses on coarse cloth, the threads drawn out so as to form squares. Each of the holes produced by drawing the threads out, is worked with coloured silk, in stripes, or squares, or zig-zag, according to fancy.

After the above-mentioned purses are finished, they are sewed into clasps, with strong waxed silk.

———

The miser's purse has neither beauty nor use: it is merely intended as a puzzle. It is made of three circular pieces of cloth; each of these pieces are cut down lengthways through the centre. Two of them, after being cut in two, are stitched up again tight in the middle; the third is kept together by loops of sewing silk, passing from end to end on the wrong side, and going through the middle, so as to unite the pieces.

This drawing represents one half of the circles as black, and the other white; people usually make the two halves of each circle of different colours. When the three circles are thus prepared, they are all joined together, so as to form a three-sided bag: the edges are bound with narrow ribbon, and bows are placed top and bottom. By pulling gently upon the side caught together with loops, it can be opened in the centre, and a bit of money squeezed in. When drawn up tight, it appears to be entirely without an entrance; and those who have never seen one, would be sadly puzzled to get the money out.

———

PEN-WIPERS.

These are a very necessary accompaniment to a neat writing-desk. The most common ones consist of two circular pieces of black velvet, neatly bound, and caught together in the middle with two or three circular pieces of black broadcloth between them, for the purpose of wiping the pens.

Some, instead of velvet covers, have bits of black broadcloth, covered with little bright-coloured round pieces, about as big as a wafer, laid one over another like the scales of a fish. The butterfly is likewise a common form. The wings are of embroidered velvet, and the leaves between are of black broadcloth.

The most convenient pen-wiper is made of three pointed pieces of broadcloth, about half of a quarter of a yard long. Each piece is about an eighth of a yard, or two nails, wide at the bottom, and goes off to a point at the top. Each one is stitched up separately, and turned wrong side outward, when it looks not unlike a tunnel. After they are made, the three are all joined together at the seams, and a tasteful little bow is placed on the top. The bottom can be bound, or embroidered with gay colours, according to fancy. This form is peculiarly convenient; because the pen can be run into these little tunnels, and wiped, without any danger of inking the fingers. Pen-wipers should always be made of black flannel, or broadcloth: other colours soon get spoiled by the ink.

———

TRIMMING, &c.

I SHALL not attempt to explain how the various kinds of trimming are made, for it is impossible to make them by any written description; but I will mention those I know—and little girls that really wish to learn, will soon find some kind sister, or aunt, or grandmother, who will gladly teach them.

Tatten is sometimes made on the fingers, and sometimes on a frame; it is button-hole stitch, drawn up into little scallops.

Daisy trimming consists of little tufts of cotton fastened on a cord at regular distances, and then cut as close as velvet.

Tape trimming is made of very narrow tape, turned in such a way as to produce a succession of points, and kept in that form by a thread run through the centre. Any child could find out how to make it by looking at a piece.

Bobbin is a four-sided kind of cord, made on a little wooden instrument, shaped like a harp, with a hole at the bottom, for the cord to pass through. This is very pretty work, and easily done.

Watch-guards are made of four strands of very, very narrow braid, woven together on the fingers, in such a manner as to produce a round cord full of little checks. A four-sided cord instead of a round one, will be produced by doing the work backward every other time. Some people leave open spaces of unwoven braid every inch, or half inch. Bracelets of ten, twelve, or more strands, may be woven after a similar fashion. I think it is impossible to make these things, without having seen some one do them.

A very pretty kind of necklace is made of black sewing silk, and small gold beads. The sewing silk is worked like button-holes, so as to produce a flat cord. It is done on a frame. Two strands are made; and every inch, or half inch, the threads of which the strands are made, are passed through four gold beads, in such a manner as to arrange them in the form of a diamond.

RUG-WORK.

LITTLE mats, for lamps, work-boxes, &c. are very easily made by children; and they are extremely pretty. They are worked on canvass, with bright-coloured worsteds. There are several stitches; one is precisely like the common marking stitch. Some have flowers, or fruit, worked in the middle, and all the spaces filled up with one colour, so as to form a ground; others are worked in slanting stripes, squares, or zig-zag; in the latter case, they look better to be worked only with two colours; and those should contrast well together, like purple and yellow, brown and orange colour, salmon colour and blue, crimson and black, &c.

The fringe is formed by sewing the worsted very thick over a round stick, and then cutting it open. Some make a very beautiful flower-fringe, by arranging their worsted in such colours and shapes, as imitate chinasters, daisies, &c.

The least interesting and the most laborious part of rug-work is filling up all the spaces, so as to form the ground-work. By the following process this can be easily avoided: take a piece of broadcloth, or cassimere, of such colour as you fancy for the ground-work, baste it under the canvass; work your flowers the same as usual, only be sure to pass all the stitches through the broadcloth; when finished, pull out all the threads of the canvass; the work will be left on the broadcloth, and will, of course, need no filling up. This saves a great deal of time, and really looks more rich.

EMBROIDERY

THIS is nearly out of fashion; and I am glad it is: for it is a sad waste of time. I call it a waste, because things so much more beautiful can be produced with so much less trouble than used to be bestowed upon tent-stitch, print-stitch, &c.

One kind is simple and easy; and if done with taste, has great beauty. I mean, chenille of various colours and shades sewed upon white satin, or silk, in imitation of flowers.

Embroidery on muslin is one of the most tasteful employments a woman can have. Skill in this depends upon practice, and a good choice of patterns is very important.

The principal caution necessary to give little girls is to draw the thread through gently, so as not to pull the muslin; and to make their leaves slender and well shaped, instead of having them thick, and all the way of a bigness. French patterns should be taken for copies, being much more beautiful than any other.

When muslin is too much worn for use, the work can be cut out and sewed upon lace with very little trouble; and if done with care, it looks as well as new work.

It requires less taste to work on lace, than on muslin; because it is all done in stitches as regular as marking. This work should never be attempted in the evening; as it is extremely injurious to the eyes. The best kind of frames consist of two little hoops, wound with flannel; one big enough to go over the other; and the lace confined between them.

MARKING.

INDELIBLE ink is now so much in use, that the general habit of marking samplers is almost done away: but like many other old-fashioned things, it is a very good thing.

There are times in everybody's life when it is convenient to know how to mark the letters of the alphabet; good taste may be shown in it, as well as in other branches of needle-work; and, at all events, it is a safe and pretty employment for idle little fingers.

PATCH-WORK.

THIS is old-fashioned too; and I must allow it is very silly to tear up large pieces of cloth, for the sake of sewing them together again. But little girls often have a great many small bits of cloth, and large remnants of time, which they don't know what to do with; and I think it is better for them to make cradle-quilts for their dolls, or their baby brothers, than to be standing round, wishing they had something to do. The pieces are arranged in a great variety of forms: squares, diamonds, stars, blocks, octagon pieces placed in circles, &c. A little girl should examine whatever kind she wishes to imitate, and cut a paper pattern, with great care and exactness.

KNITTING.

THIS favourite employment of our grandmothers ought not to be forgotten. It enables one to be useful in the decline of life, when they can no longer be actively useful; and it is a never-failing amusement. I never knew an old lady ignorant of it, who did not deeply regret she had never learned. Independent of these considerations, a little girl ought to know how to do *everything ;* it may not always be necessary for her to sew and knit—but she should *know how.* Many know the stitch of knitting very well, who are entirely ignorant how to shape a stocking. The stitches should be cast on double yarn, two stitches taken up through each loop. After knitting eight or ten times round, you should turn directly back, and knit on the wrong side ; this makes a little elastic roll, which serves to make the stockings strong at the top : some prefer seaming every two stitches, thinking it is stronger than the roll. Gentlemen's stockings should always be seamed three or four inches from the top : they are not narrowed at all, until the heel is nearly finished; but ladies' stockings should be narrowed seven or eight times, after four or five inches have been knit from the top. The narrowing should be done on each side the seaming needle ; and five or six bouts knit between each time. A bout is once going round ; a pearl is twice round. A long heel makes a better shaped stocking than a short one ; especially if gores are knit into the sides. Gores are knit in the following manner: knit round the foot of the stocking once, and narrow at the beginning of one side-needle, and the end of the other. The second time going round, knit through the instep-needle, knit two stitches on the side-needle, narrow, hen turn back, and knit the instep-needle on the wrong side, just as you did in knitting the heel; knit two stitches in the same way from the side-needle, and narrow; slip the stitch you have narrowed back upon the side-needle, and knit on the other two, which belong there; then turn back and knit round the stocking after the usual manner. This knitting the instep-needle twice, where you knit the others once, will produce a hole each time; but narrowing the last double-knit stitch with one from the side-needles, every time you go round, remedies the evil. The first side you knit, after leaving the instep, knit two stitches, and narrow by slipping one stitch under the other at the last side-needle, leave four, and take wo stitches up together.

The heel must contain just half the stitches in the whole stocking. When nearly done, it must be narrowed seven or eight times before it is bound together, by placing its two halves side by side, and knitting two stitches together, with a third needle. Some finish it differently; they take just half the stitches of the heel in the middle of the needle, leaving a quarter on one side, and a quarter on the other; they knit the middle only; but each time they take up one stitch from the side, and narrow it with one on the middle, until all the side stitches are gone. The foot is formed by taking up two loops on each side of the heel; before these are knit, the side-needles should be widened, by taking up an additional loop at the end of every three stitches; it should then be narrowed at the corner of the side-needles until the foot is small enough. The toe may be formed by dividing the stitches in such a way that half will be on the instep-needle, and a quarter on each of the others; knit two stitches at the beginning of the instep-needle, and then narrow by slipping one of the two next stitches under the other; at the end, leave four stitches, and narrow, by taking up two stitches at once; slip and bind in the same way at the beginning of one side-needle; and narrow by taking up two at once, at the end of the other. A more common way is to narrow every seven stitches when you begin the toe; knit seven bouts, and narrow every seven stitches again; knit six bouts, and narrow every six stitches; knit five bouts, and narrow every five stitches; and so on.

Whoever knows how to knit a stocking, cannot help finding out how to knit a mitten, if they look at one.

There is a kind of knitting, called pegging, done by drawing the yarn through every loop with one crooked ivory needle. Little woollen shoes for infants are knit a great deal in this way; likewise suspenders. A very elastic kind of suspenders is made by knitting one stitch and slipping the next upon the needle without knitting, casting the yarn directly over it. The next time going round, this stitch and its loop are knit together, and the stitches which were knit before are slipped, and a loop thrown over them.

The open-work knitting is made by taking up a loop between the stitches, taking care to narrow immediately after, to prevent your work from growing wide. These holes may be formed into any figures you fancy. Some people knit their names into stockings in this way, forming the letters just as they would in marking.

Netting is simple and pretty work, done with a small ivory needle made for the purpose. It consists merely in tying threads together in diamonds. Silk nets were formerly used for the hair; but at present, coarse nets for the fisherman and the cook, are the only ones in use.

BEES.

These busy little insects are the most interesting creatures in the world. If they cared anything about our good opinion, it would certainly make them very happy to know how much has been said and written about them in all ages; but like all clever people, they have too much to do to attend to their own affairs, to afford time for inquiring what their neighbours say.

It is a pleasant thing to have a hive of these busy interesting insects in a sheltered nook of the garden. They afford a perpetual lesson of industry and neatness; and it is impossible to watch their operations without thinking of that all-wise God, who has bestowed upon them such wonderful instincts.

When a swarm has been lodged in a hive, it is observed that the bees hastily arrange themselves into four divisions: one leaves the hive to range the fields in search of materials for the commencement of their work; another party carefully examine the hive, and close every opening save those by which they enter and leave their habitation; the third band of workers lay the foundation of the cells, by ejecting and moulding the wax formed in their stomachs; while the fourth finish neatly what the others have begun.

The workers are constantly employed in gathering the pollen of flowers, and in forming the waxen cells. Their hind legs are provided with little baskets, by means of which they carry home their store of pollen to the hive. Here is the picture of a working bee:

The queen bee is the mother of the whole colony. The happiness and welfare of the hive seem to depend entirely upon her. One only is allowed to be in a hive; and her cell is easily distinguished by its great size. If any accident happens to her, the workers mournfully give up their customary labours. So great is their affection, that when the queen is sick, they wait upon her with the tender assiduity of anxious nurses. Here is a picture of the queen bee:

The drones are never seen abroad upon the flowers: they stay at home, and live on the industry of the workers. Here is a likeness of one of the lazy things:

Bees, in the formation of their cells, observe the most curious mathematical exactness. The cells are hexagonal, or six-sided, and constructed on a principle that at once affords the most room, and consumes the least possible quantity of wax. The most learned mathematician could not have contrived it better. The comb consists of a double row of cells, so placed that the base of one cell serves likewise for the one opposite.

To prevent these delicate cells from being worn out by the multitude of little feet all the time passing over them, they take the precaution to make a rim round the margin of each, four times thicker than the walls. The insect labours with its jaws, making the work compact and smooth by repeated strokes. The engraving represents one side of a honey-comb, and the royal cell of a queen bee, which has been opened:

The hive of bees should not be exposed to a hot sun, and should be well sheltered from cold winds. The place must be retired, and near a running stream, if possible; for they are remarkably fond of quiet, and of pure water. Among flowers, they love best the crocus, the buc' `···
clover; but above all, the sweet-scented mig

Their stings, when seen through a microscope, resemble a double-headed arrow. They never attack a person unless they are irritated in some way. When swarming, they are sometimes enraged by an attempt to brush them from the place where they have alighted. The hiving of bees is not a dangerous business for those who have experience in it; but children should never think of attempting it. Numerous stings occasion great pain, and sometimes cause death. Chalk, with spirits of hartshorn, is a useful remedy applied to the injured part. Common salt, wet and put upon the wound, is likewise very good. The pain is occasioned by a drop of liquid from a little bag of poison, with which the bee is provided for his defence. When persons are stung, if they will wait till the bee withdraws the sting, the wound will not be near so painful, as if the insect were driven off; in which case, the bag of venom, as well as the sting, remain in the wound.

When a bee loses his sting in this way, it never grows again: and he soon dies of the injury.

The working bees in one hive often amount to from 15,000 to 30,000, or more. They kill all the *drones* in the month of September, which is an easy work, as they have no stings. When the bees of one hive have become too numerous, they separate, and a new swarm, headed by a queen, fly off to seek another establishment. In winter, they feed on the honey stored during the warm season. In the coldest days, they are nearly torpid, but never for any length of time.

Wild bees were formerly very common in New-England; and they are sometimes found now. They make their nests usually in the trunks of old trees. The hunters have a curious way of tracing them to their homes. They catch a bee, and after holding it some time, they let it fly, and observe which way it steers its course; this betrays in what direction the nest is. They then catch another bee, move about a hundred rods off, and let it fly: the angle or point where the two lines would meet, is the place of the nest. Here is an engraving to explain it; it represents three bees flying home from three different points:

The Humble-Bee forms an intermediate link between the Hive-Bee and the Wasp. Their honey is said to be more delicious than that of the hive-bee. When there is a scarcity of food, the hive-bees sometimes go and rob the nests of the humble-bees; and it is said that these amiable little creatures, returning home with a load, have been persuaded to part with all the contents of their honey-bags, and then patiently fly away for more. They make their nests under ground, by the corner of some old fence, or the trunk of a decayed tree. Their winter apartments are comfortably lined with moss. Here is one of these happy little societies.

There are various kinds of bees called Solitary Bees, because they do not live together in societies, or hives. One is called the Mason Bee, because she builds her nest of sand and little stones glued together; another is called the Mining Bee, on account of its digging chambers for itself under ground; then there is the Carpenter Bee, which saws its way into soft wood, and forms a nest; and the Upholsterer Bee, which nips pieces out of rose leaves, wherewith she makes pretty curtains to line her cell. The Carder Bee, which heckles moss to form her habitations, is not solitary. They join together in a file to perform their task; the last bee lays hold of some of the moss with her mandibles, disentangles it from the rest, and having *carded* it with her fore legs into a small bundle, she pushes it under her body to the next bee, who passes it in the same manner; and so on, till it is brought to the border of the nest.

Is it any wonder that these extraordinary little insects are objects of so much interest to mankind? Their ingenuity has been a subject of admiration in all ages, and their industry has afforded a proverb to the moralist, and a text to the preacher, from the earliest times. Several philosophers have spent nearly their whole lives in watching them. Some have called them "winged mathematicians," and others, "the little confectioners of nature." "They are often noticed in the Scriptures; and Palestine is, you know, repeatedly described as 'a land flowing with honey.' In truth, nearly the whole of Syria affords large quantities of this luscious food; the bees make their cells in hollow trees, and in the crevices of the rocks; the numerous wild flowers of the country afford them ample means for storing their cells. The forests of Hungary also yield such large quantities, that it is almost a staple of the country. The mountains of Turkey, in Europe, swarm with bees; and you may remember that Hymettis, especially, owes its celebrity to this article. Caffraria produces abundance of wild honey; and the means by which the inhabitants discover the nests is so singular, that I must relate it to you. There is in their forests a small bird called the Bee-cuckoo, Moroc, or Honey-guide; it is about the size of the sparrow, of an ash colour, a little variegated with yellow and white. The Moroc is remarkably fond of honey, and of the young bee-worms; but cannot itself invade the nests, fearing by instinct, the attacks of the large bees. There is also in that country a small animal of the weasel tribe, called the Ratel, or Honey-weasel. This creature has a remarkably tough skin, by which it is defended from the attacks of the bees, whose nests it breaks up; thus preventing the dangerous increase of these numerous swarms of insects. Towards night, the Ratel leaves his burrow, and watches the direction and flight of the bees which, at this hour, are congregating to their cells. He is thus almost certain of tracing them, and when found, feasts himself with impunity on their delicious stores. But he is also taught by sagacity to follow the Moroc, which leads the way to the bee-nests, uttering at the same time a loud shrill note. While the Ratel devours the honey, the Moroc secures her share of the plunder, and makes a hearty meal of what her companion rejects. The Hottentots, accustomed to the way of these animals, are enabled, by noticing their movements, to take large quantities of honey without much labour: they always leave some for the little bird which guides them to the bee-nests."

SILK-WORMS.

THESE insects are perhaps more serviceable than any other to mankind. Nearly half the world are clothed with the web they spin from their own bodies! They abound in China more than in any other place; it is generally supposed they were brought into Europe from that country; the ancient name of China signified "the country of silk."

At Rome, in the time of Aurelian, silk was sold for its weight in gold; now almost every body has at least one silk gown. The eggs which produce the worm are hatched in May or June, unless artificial heat brings them out at an earlier period. The eggs are no bigger than mustard-seed; and the worms, when first hatched, are very small; but they feed on fresh mulberry leaves so voraciously, that in six or seven weeks they grow to the size represented in the engraving.

When they are growing, they shed their coats several times, each time assuming more delicate and beautiful colours. They have nine holes on each side, through which they breathe. The silk is spun from two small sacks on each side filled with a gummy substance, which becomes silky as it dries. The worm never breaks his thread as he spins; and it is said one ball contains entire silk enough to reach six miles. These balls are called cocoons; the engraving represents one of them.

These answer the same purpose as the chrysalis of the butterfly; and if they were let alone, a delicate white moth, or miller, would eat its way out of each of them; but the hole thus eaten would break the silk in pieces; therefore they bake or scald them, in order to kill the moths. Those that are reserved for eggs are laid away in dark, still places, on sheets of paper. The moth comes out of the cocoon, lays her eggs, and dies immediately.

A few minutes' attention each day, for six or seven weeks, is all that is necessary to be bestowed upon these industrious little things. One person can attend to fifty thousand, without difficulty. It takes 2300 worms to produce a pound of silk. The principal thing is to keep every thing about them very clean and sweet. They must have fresh mulberry leaves two or three times a day; and they must not be covered with dew, dried in the hot sun, or impregnated with any disagreeable smell. Some young ladies sprinkle the leaves to keep them fresh; this is almost sure to make the worm sicken and die.

In China, a woman has the care of the silk establishments, who is called "The Mother of the Worms." She is never allowed to enter the room, without previously washing her hands, and putting on clean clothes. Every year, the Empress celebrates a great feast in honour of the silk-worms; during which, she and all the great ladies of the court march in procession, carrying branches of the mulberry tree.

There are several species of wild silk-worms in China, whose web is stronger and coarser than that of the cultivated ones. Wild cocoons are gray; those cultivated here are of a beautiful straw colour.

The Chinese children are much employed in the manufactories of silk. Indeed, they are brought up always to be busy about something or other. A gentleman just returned from Canton, told me he never saw the children at play there; that they all look like little old men and women, whose minds were mighty full of business. I should like to send them a book of games—should'nt you? I think "all work and no play, makes Jack a dull boy."

ON KEEPING ANIMALS.

It is a good rule to keep only such animals as are happier for being domesticated; such as kittens, dogs, or pet lambs. I would not keep a robin shut up in a cage, for the price of fifty birds. Do what you can for him, you cannot make him half so happy as he would be abroad among the sunshine and the flowers. Canary birds must be kept in the house; because they came from the warm islands of Canary. And it would kill them to expose them to our winter; but, kind little reader, if you have any feathered prisoners, which belong to our own climate, I beg of you to open the door and let them fly the first bright day the next spring. I have likewise an objection to keeping rabbits and squirrels; because I am sure they are not so happy as they would be in their native woods.

If birds are kept, their cages should be carefully cleaned every day; and they should be well supplied with fresh seed and clean water. Their cage should be hung in a warm, shady nook, out of the reach of their old enemy, the cat. Gold fishes should have pure water every day, and be kept very clean. The water should not be intensely cold. If rabbits are kept, their habitations should likewise be kept perfectly clean. The door should be closely grated with wire, so that it may at once be safe, and let in the pure air; there should be two apartments, one for sleeping, and one for eating, communicating with each other by a round hole, large enough for the rabbit to jump through; the edges of this hole and of the door should be lined with tin, otherwise the rabbit will nibble them with his sharp teeth. The box should slightly tip backward, that it may be kept perfectly dry. Rabbits love clover, lettuce, and lady's delights. Little girls should never feed animals with any new food, without asking advice of those who are experienced. Birds and rabbits are often killed in this way.

MY BIRD.

My pretty bird ! it makes me sad
   To think thou canst not fly ;
For well I know thou would'st be glad
   To see the bright blue sky.

Every day we bring thee seed,
   Myself and sister Mary ;
For dearly do we love to feed
   Our favourite Canary.

And very oft we slily creep,
   When he has ceased to sing,
To see the pretty dear asleep,
   With head beneath his wing.

But he's not happy in our love—
  The poor imprisoned thing!
He longs across the fields to rove,
  And stretch his weary wing.

Indeed, indeed, I'd let him go,
  And never say one word,
Were I not sure the wind and snow
  Would kill my bonny bird.

They brought him here from distant isles,
  Where the days are long and bright ;
Where earth is warm with sunny smiles,
  And zephyrs fan the night.

By the first good ship across the main,
  We'll send him to Canary ;
And we'll ne'er keep a bird again—
  Say—will you, sister Mary ?

GARDENING.

PERHAPS there is no amusement in the world that combines health, instruction, and pleasure, so much as gardening. The fresh air, and the smell of the earth, makes the little gardener strong and rosy; the growth of the flowers, with their infinite variety of forms and colours, is a never-failing source of pleasure; while the wonderful formation of seed—the bees who dive into the flowers for the load of honey—the leaf-cutting insect, which so adroitly cuts from them lining and curtains for his little nest—the leaf-roller, that fastens its spider-web cables upon the edge of the leaf, and then pulls and pulls, until he rolls it into the form he wants—all these, and a hundred other things, which an attentive little girl would observe, yield abundance of instruction, and fill us with wonder and gratitude to an all-wise and merciful God.

To enjoy this employment, or derive benefit from it, you

should try to find out the reason of every thing you observe; for there *is* a reason for every thing in nature, whether we discover it or not. Do you wish to know why the dandelion has a winged seed? Why those of the burr are hooked? Why the balsamine and the country-artillery explode at a touch? I will tell you. All flowers, in their natural state, grow wild in the woods, in some country or other. Those we have in our gardens are generally brought from foreign countries; we carefully gather the seeds of our garden-flowers; but there is nobody to gather them in the woods; and God, to prevent any thing he has made from being lost, provides the wild-flowers with means to plant themselves. The dandelion, by means of its little downy wing, is carried through the air, and planted in every direction; the burr clings to every thing that touches it, and is thus transported from one place to another; if an insect rests on the balsamine, its seed-vessels contract and burst, and the seeds are scattered, as if from a pop-gun.

Bulbs are another wonderful provision for plants that cannot endure the cold. They are not roots, but little subterranean nests, in which the plants lie folded up, till the warm sun comes to visit them. The fibres, that shoot from the bottom of the bulbs, are the real roots. In hot countries, very few native plants are provided with bulbs, because they do not need them.

A little girl does not deserve the name of a gardener, unless she actually takes care of her own garden, and has no assistance except in such work as is either dirty or very fatiguing

I know some young ladies, who have a garden, and *call* it their own; but they neither plant it, nor weed it, nor water it, nor gather the seeds—perhaps they do not even know the names of their plants, and in what month they blossom.

Now this is no gardening at all. You should gather the seed yourself, in a dry time, when you are sure they are perfectly ripe: for if they are put away damp, they will mou d. They should be done up in strong paper, carefully folded, that they may not be spilt. On the outside should be neatly written the *name* of the plant, what *month* it is in flower, and how *high* it is. In this way, you will be able to plant low flowers on the margin of your beds where they can be easily seen, instead of having them entirely hidden among tall plants; and by knowing the time they blossom, you can plant some for every month in each part of your garden, and thus keep it in bloom all the season.

TO PRODUCE VARIOUS FLOWERS FROM ONE STEM.

Scoor the pith from a small twig of elder; split it lengthways, and fill each of the parts with seeds that produce different coloured flowers. Surround the seed with earth; tie the two bits of wood together; and plant the whole in a pot filled with earth. The stems of the different plants will thus be so incorporated, as to exhibit to the eye only one stem, throwing out branches with the different flowers you have planted. By choosing the seeds of plants which germinate at the same period, and which are nearly similar in the texture of their stems, an intelligent person may obtain artificial plants extremely curious.

TO PRESERVE ROSES TILL CHRISTMAS.

WHEN roses are budding and blooming, is the time to lay by a treat for Christmas. Select from your rose trees such buds as are just ready to blow: tie a piece of fine thread round the stalk of each; do not handle the bud, or the stalk; cut it from the tree with the stalk two or three inches in length; melt sealing-wax, and quickly apply it to the end of the stalk; the wax should only be just warm enough to be ductile; form a piece of paper into a cone-like shape, wherein place the rose; twist it at the ends to exclude the air; put it in a box, and put the box into a drawer: this is to be sure that the air is excluded. In winter, take it out, cut off the end of the stalk, place it in lukewarm water, and in two or three hours it will have the freshness and fragrance of summer. If the room is very warm, it will answer to put it in cold water.

THE FADED ROSE RESTORED.

THROW some sulphur on a chafing-dish of hot coals, hold a faded rose over the fumes of the sulphur, and it will become quite white; in this state dip it into water; put it into a box, or drawer, for three or four hours; when taken out, it will be quite red again.

MAY MORNING.

THIS is an innocent and pretty festival for children. The only objection to it is, that May is a cold month in our climate; and the first day is very apt to be wet, windy, or stormy. In America, we should celebrate the first of June, instead of the first of May; then we should be sure of plenty of flowers, and have a fair chance of bright weather.

In Greece and Rome, they always kept a festival as soon as spring began to appear, in honour of Flora, the goddess of flowers.

At the same season, in ancient times, the English used to form long processions, carrying green boughs, and leading oxen decorated with flowers; they stopped and danced round a tall May-pole hung with garlands; the little girls still crown their favourite companion Queen of May, and carry baskets of flowers to their companions. I like this custom. It used to make me very happy to receive a basket of violets, and a verse of poetry, from my scholars. There is something amiable and polite in such little attentions.

Some make the May-crown of cardboard, bound with gilt paper, to resemble a king's crown; but a simple wreath of wild flowers, tied in clusters, is far prettier. Baskets of white pasteboard, bound with pink, or blue taste, are strong enough. Those made with deep scolloped edges, to roll over, and fasten on the sides, are pretty; moss may be sewed on to give them a rural appearance; but a great quantity would be too heavy for baskets of such frail materials. Here are some verses suitable to put among the flowers.

> Anemonies, violets, cowslips for you,
> Fresh from the pastures, all sparkling with dew;
> Then, lady, twine them round thy brow,
> And be as blithe as we are now.

Nature's rich carpet now is spread—
The young vines spring beneath her tread
This wild-flower wreath we bring to thee,
In honour of her Jubilee!

The blue bird now begins to sing,
The insect spreads his tiny wing;
And children too are very gay,
To welcome in delightful May!

"All the goodly things that be
In earth, and air, and ample sea,
Are waking up to welcome thee,
Thou lovely month of May!"

MISCELLANEOUS.

THE SELF-SATISFIED DUCK.—A FABLE.
Translated from the Spanish.

A Duck waddling from a muddy pond, thus sounded her own praises as she went: "What animal has such extraordinary gifts as myself? I am confined to no element: I can walk on the earth, swim in the water, and fly in the air. On no other creature has nature lavished such various talents!" A wise old cow that was feeding near the pond, thus reproved the vanity of the duck: "Let me tell you, Mistress Duck

that you talk like a foolish, ignorant thing, as you are. It is
true you can walk, swim, and fly; but *how* do you do all these
things? Why, in honest truth, you do them all so badly, that
it is enough to make one laugh to look upon you. When you
can swim as well as the beautiful dolphin, run with the fleet-
ness of the nimble deer, or cut the air as rapidly as the graceful swallow—then you may, with some reason, talk of your
various talents; but at present, you will be least likely to be
ridiculed, if you remain silent."

MORAL. There is small merit in knowing how to do a
little of every thing, provided one does nothing well.

————

THE UMBRELLA, THE MUFF, AND THE FAN.
Translated from the Spanish.

AN umbrella, lying on the table with a muff and a fan, thus
addressed them: "How strange it is that you do not learn to
accommodate yourselves to circumstances, instead of being fit
for certain times, and certain places, only. You, Miss Fan,
are used merely for a few bright, warm, summer days, and are
then thrown by. You, Mrs. Muff, are hid in a corner until
the cold and stormy winter comes; and when the cheerful
sun shows his face, you are considered an incumbrance.
But I am used at all seasons of the year—I protect man from
the rains and snows of winter; and I likewise shield him from
the too ardent sun of summer."

MORAL. We should early learn what is useful, without neglecting elegance and grace, that we may adorn any situation in which we happen to be placed. A knowledge of useful things will enable us to bear poverty more cheerfully; while elegant acquirements will serve to dignify and adorn prosperity.

ADDRESS TO MY KITTEN.

My pretty kitten, mild and meek,
Stretch'd in the sunshine, still and sleek,
One would judge, by your sober grace,
You did no worse than wash your face!

You take wondrous care of your glossy fur,
And keep time, meanwhile, with a drowsy purr,
As if you despised the vulgar old cats,
That jump on their feet at the sound of rats.

But, sly Miss Kit, I know you well!
You need not act the languid belle—
For you and I have romp'd together,
Through ev'ry sort of wind and weather.

Who goes to the pantry, to steal new milk?
Who upsets my box, and tangles my silk?
Who chases leaves in the autumn gale?
And who frisks about for her own gray tail?

It is a truth, you're wild and young—
Like me—without my rattling tongue—
And mother says, my little treasure,
That youth is but a fleeting pleasure.

Time soon will change you to a dull old cat—
Yet how little you seem to think of that!
But a woman, you know, must be more wise
Than a puss, too old to catch butterflies.

So, Kit, 'tis plain that you and I
Shall be compell'd to say good-bye!
But come—let's have another play—
I shan't be nine till New-Year's day.

MARY HOWARD.

MARY HOWARD was the daughter of wealthy parents in England. They loved her very much, and were willing to grant every wish of her little heart. Indeed, all around her became extremely attached to her; she was so quiet and affectionate, and looked so much like a little dove.

She always wanted to share every thing she had with others. As soon as she could speak, she would carry her box of sugar-plums from one to another, saying, "Mamma, too"— "Papa, too"—"Nurse, too." She was so tender-hearted, that one day, when the cat mewed because she had pulled her fur, she ran and hid her head in her mother's lap, and grieved sadly; when her mother wiped her eyes and kissed her, she tried to look cheerful; but as soon as she saw puss, her little lips puckered again, and she would sob out, " *Mamy* hurt kitty—kitty *ky.*"

No wonder this sweet child was the darling of the whole house. She was indeed tended with as much care as her own pet lamb, whose neck she every day dressed with fresh flowers. But a sad, sad change, was in store for poor Mary! Her father was thrown from his carriage, and killed suddenly. She saw him brought into the house, and laid upon his bed, and she cried bitterly, because he did not speak to her; but she did not know he was dead. After they had put him in the tomb, it almost broke her mother's heart to hear the questions she

asked.   When told that her father had gone to heaven, where
God would take care of him, she asked, " What made him go,
mother ? We loved him—why did he not stay with us ?" And
when her mother told her that God made good people happy
in another world, she said with great earnestness, " But he
won't have any little Mary there, to kiss."   She was not old
enough then to know, that when we die, we only go to the
home God has provided for us ; that the good, who are left on
earth, may grieve, but that the good, who have gone before
them, are happy.   Her mother told her all this ; but it was too
big for her little mind to understand.

Before a year had passed away, Mrs. Howard died of con-
sumption ; and poor little Mary was left an orphan, without
brother or sister.   Oh! then it was a heart-breaking sight to
see the little creature roaming about the house, now sitting
down in a corner to sob all alone, and now running to hide
her head in nurse's lap, and begging to go to heaven, where
she could see her father and mother.   Mary had but two rela-
tions in the wide world ; one was her mother's brother, who
lived in Calcutta ; the other, her father's brother.   The latter
was appointed her guardian.   He was very wicked.   He did
not love his gentle and pretty niece ; for he wanted his
brother's wealth ; and he knew that if she were dead, he
should have large houses, and plenty of silver, and gold, and
jewels.   The more he thought of these things, the more he
hated the lovely child, who had been placed under his care by

her dying parents; for if we let bad thoughts stay in our minds, they grow stronger and stronger every hour. One by one, this wicked man dismissed all the old domestics, and then he carried Mary away in a carriage, saying he was going to live in a country-house a great many miles from London.

The old nurse wept bitterly at parting with her darling. She offered to go and live with her without wages; and when the cruel uncle denied this, her heart misgave her that all was not right. Not long after, this faithful domestic heard the news that Mary Howard was lost—that the gipsies had stolen her, for the sake of an amber necklace, which was around her neck, when she was last seen. Betty Morris, (that was the nurse's name) did not believe this story. She believed the uncle had killed her, for the sake of the silver and gold; and Betty wrote as good a letter as she could to Mary's uncle in Calcutta, and told him all that happened, and how much she felt afraid that his sister's orphan had fallen into cruel hands.

But Calcutta is a great distance from London—it would take many, many months, for an answer to return to Betty's letter—and what was to be done for poor little Mary all this time? Mortals could not do any thing to help her; but when I have told you my story, you will see how her Heavenly Father took care of her.

Mr. Howard was indeed as wicked as Betty suspected. By promises of large sums of money, he persuaded a poor sailor to drown the child. This sailor had a soft heart; but he had not been taught when young, to remember that the eye of God was upon all his actions.

He wanted money very much; and not having the fear of God before his eyes, he thought to make himself rich by drowning a helpless orphan. He coaxed her away from her uncle's house by means of a new doll; and then, when he pretended he was carrying her back again, he was conveying her afar off, into Wales. Mary was then only four years old; and the country was all new to her; she did not know where she was going; she cried sometimes, but a few words of kindness soon comforted her. By her loving and quiet ways, she gained upon the rough sailor's affections; and when he looked on her black dress, and thought how she was left all alone in the world, he covered his face with his hands, and prayed in his heart, " God forgive me, for ever thinking to do her wrong." One day he led her down on the sea-beach to gather shells. The sight of the water made him shudder—for he thought of his own wicked intentions; and while he was thinking of these things, Mary, who had hold of his hand, looked up in his face, and said, "Where are you going? Is this the way home?" "Where do you want to go?" asked the sailor. "I should like to go to heaven," answered the innocent child; "for father and mother have gone there, and nobody loves Mary now." "Bless your blue eyes!" exclaimed the sailor, "Robert loves you!" and caught her in his arms, and wept over her, as if she had been his own.

Robert did not know what to do with his little treasure. Sometimes he thought he would leave her in the street—" But then," said he, " perhaps the sweet little creature will starve." He ought to have gone back to London with her, and made known her uncle's wickedness to some of her father's old friends ; but he was afraid to do that—for Mr. Howard was a powerful man, and Robert did not dare to offend him. At last, he concluded he would take her to sea with him ; and having engaged a passage in a ship bound to New-Zealand, he took her on board. For a few days, Mary was very unhappy ; and when they asked her why she cried, she would say she wanted to see father and mother, and Betty Morris, and her white lamb, and her kitten. A sailor's life was a hard life for one brought up so carefully and delicately as little Mary had been ; but she was at an age when kindness was all the wealth she wanted ; and Robert grew so very fond of her, that he could not bear to have her out of his sight a moment. He pretended that she was his child, and that her mother was dead. Thus you see how people who do one wicked thing, are led to another. My little readers, if you want to *conceal* anything you are about to do, you may be sure there is something *wrong* in it. When you are tempted to do what you are not quite sure is right, kneel and pray earnestly that your Father in heaven would keep you from *beginning* to sin.

The ship in which Mary sailed was named the Sea-bird There was on board a savage boy, the son of a New-Zealand

Chief, whose name was Duaterra. His father had agreed that he should work for the Captain, to pay his passage to England and back again. He had been to London, and was now on his way home to his native island. One day, he was so very lazy and saucy, that the Captain ordered him to be flogged, in order to teach him better manners. Duaterra was very angry. He thought it was a great insult to treat the son of a Chief in such a shameful manner.

New-Zealanders are savages: very much like what our North-American Indians used to be. When they think any one has done them an injury, they always seek revenge for it, by doing an injury in return; for they never have read in the Holy Bible, that men should love and forgive one another. Duaterra did not tell his thoughts; but he resolved in his own heart to kill all on board, except Robert and his little Mary. " I will not kill Robert," said he to himself, " because he gave me a Turkish pipe, and always shares his biscuit with me; and as for little mocking-bird Mary, I would not have her killed for all the pipes in the world." He called her mocking-bird, because she made him laugh, by trying to repeat all the words he spoke to her. You see how orphan Mary made friends wherever she went. It was all because she was so gentle and affectionate, so careful not to make any trouble, and so willing to do whatever was pleasing to others. She was the favourite plaything of every one on board.

After a long voyage, they arrived at New-Zealand. Duaterra

still laid up in his heart the remembrance of the whipping he had received. He told his father of it, and made him promise to kill every one on board, except Robert and his child. One day, when they were all on shore, the Chief sounded a great sea-shell, that hung upon his arm, and the savages gathered round him in great numbers, and rushed on the white people and killed them. Duaterra stood by a tree, with his arms round Robert and Mary; and no harm came on them When all the others were dead, the New-Zealanders plundered the Sea-Bird, and then set it on fire.

Poor little Mary clung to Robert, and screamed. It made her heart ache even to see a kitten abused: and when she saw the captain and the sailors, who had all been so kind to her, killed by the savages, it seemed as if she would have died with terror and grief. For years afterward, it always made her turn pale to speak about it.

The inhabitants of New-Zealand looked so strong and fierce, that our gentle little Mary was very much afraid of them; and she would often scream in her sleep, when she dreamed of them.

They were indeed frightful-looking creatures. They had their faces tattooed all over with strange marks; they wore their hair tied very tight on the top of their heads; and had great coarse mats hanging over their shoulders.

I suppose you will think Mary must have been very wretched here. But it is not natural for little children to be wretched long at a time. The savages were all kind to her, and Robert took as good care of her as he could. Then the island was a bright and beautiful island. There were pretty shells and gaudy flowers in plenty—and the air was full of the music of birds!*

These little feathered beauties were so very tame, that they would sometimes light on Mary's shoulder, and sing in her very ear. Hour after hour would Robert sit on the grass, and amuse his little favourite by throwing out a string, and catching the parrots as they came hopping and chattering about them; and after Mary had played with them a little while, she would let them go off to the trees again. The reason the birds are so tame there, is because the New-Zealanders have no guns and no bird-cages. The wild creatures of the woods would never be afraid of man, if he did not hurt them. All the creatures in Paradise loved Adam: and he was afraid of none of them.

Mary slept in a miserable hut, and wore a mat over her shoulders, instead of having the damask-covered bed, and neat little dresses her mother used to make for her; but she was happy, for all that. The birds and the butterflies, and the flowers, and sunshine, all made her cheerful; and the poor little creature had suffered so much, that she had almost forgotten the blessed days when she fed her own pet lamb with

---

* Captain Cooke says, the birds of New-Zealand excelled all the music he ever heard; that their notes seemed like small bells, exquisitely tuned.

milk, and dressed his neck with flowers from her own little garden.

As she grew older, she learned to carve in wood and bone, and to do shell-work, and to make baskets of various coloured bark; for in all these things the savages were very skilful.

Robert consented to be tattooed, and put white feathers on the top of his head, and married the Chief's daughter, and became himself a Chief.

Do you know what tattooing is? It is a manner of marking the skin, common in all savage nations. They cut the face with sharp instruments, and while the blood is flowing, they put in charcoal and water, which makes black lines all over the countenance. Savages consider this a great beauty; but it looks very frightful to us. Duaterra wanted to tattoo little Mary's face; but Robert would not consent to it; for in his heart he resolved to send her back to England, the first good chance he could get. Robert was now Duaterra's brother, because he had married his sister.

Duaterra did tattoo one side of Mary's forehead, notwithstanding Robert had forbidden it; and when Robert blamed him for it, he said she was going to be his little wife, and he would tattoo her face all over, if he pleased.

This reply made Robert very anxious. He could not bear the thoughts of parting with his darling; but he was determined she should never marry a savage.

When Mary was about eight years old, a wonderful opportunity occurred for sending her home. An English ship, called the Water-Witch, put in at New-Zealand to obtain fresh water—and who do you think happened to be in that vessel? One of Robert's old shipmates, named John Morris—and he was Betty Morris's own brother!

So Robert told him the whole story—how he had been hired to drown the child—and how the Lord softened his heart, that he could not do it—and how they had been saved, when all the crew of the Sea-Bird were murdered—and lastly, he told him how anxious he was to get the child back to London, for fear Duaterra would make her his wife. John Morris agreed to take care of her, and deliver her safely into the hands of her old nurse Betty.

Robert did not know how to write; but he folded up the tattered remains of the black gown Mary wore when he first took her away, and he sent that to Betty Morris, as a proof that she was indeed her own little Mary Howard.

Mary was carried on board the Water-Witch at midnight, when she was fast asleep; and Robert cried like a child, when he stood over her and looked for the last time upon her innocent little face. "Be kind to her," said he, as he wrung John Morris's hand—"for she is a precious child; and God will bless those who take care of her."

And now, the poor orphan was again cut off from all her friends, and placed entirely among strangers. For many days, she refused to be comforted, and begged all the time to go back to Robert and Duaterra.

The Captain knew nothing about her, only that she was of the two saved from the massacre of the Sea-Bird's crew. Robert had paid for her passage, with some of the money given him by her wicked uncle; for money was of no use to him in New-Zealand, and he kept it buried in the ground. John Morris was charged to keep the secret, which Robert had entrusted to him, until Mary was in safe hands; for he feared that her wicked uncle would again get the helpless child into his power.

John did his duty faithfully. As soon as they arrived in London, he bought some decent clothes for Mary, in order, as he said, to make her look more like a little Christian—and he sent off to Devonshire, where Betty lived, begging her to come to London very quick, as if life and death depended upon her speed. Betty did not know what to think of such a message; but she thought John must have some very good reason for it; and she begged her mistress to let her go. In the mean while, John had to pay his own board, and the child's board too, beside paying the messenger who went post-haste into Devonshire; for John promised Robert that he would not leave Mary a single day, until he found a better protector for her. When their money was nearly gone, Mary, who was always thoughtful and considerate, said, "John, I know how

to carve boxes, and weave baskets—don't you think the people in London would buy them of the little New-Zealand girl?"

John said it was a lucky thought, and just like her own dear
little self. So she carved a parcel of card-cases and boxes,
and John led her round the streets to sell them.

When people heard the story of the Sea-Bird, and were told
how this little girl had been saved, every body was anxious to
buy her boxes and baskets. She could not make them half
fast enough. She was called the "sailor's orphan;" for John
did not tell who she was, for fear her wicked uncle would
come for her.

At last, Betty Morris arrived in London. She said she
should have known her little favourite, "for all she had grown
so large, and was tanned, and had that shameful tattooing on
one temple;" and when she saw the little black silk frock, she
jumped and laughed, and cried, and clapped her hands, like
a crazy woman; for poor Betty Morris was so glad, she did
not know what she did.

When she became a little more calm, she said, " I can see
a Providence in it all. Her uncle Dallas came home from
Calcutta, a year ago; and he has offered ten thousand pounds
to any one who will bring him his sister's lost child." " Dallas!" exclaimed John; " that's the East-India Nabob who
bought some of Mary's carved boxes yesterday; and when I
told him the story of the sailor's orphan, he told me to bring
the child to his house in Berkeley square? I did not tel him

Mary's name; and it is little he's thinking now who is coming to see him this day."

＊　＊　＊　＊　＊　＊　＊　＊　＊

You may be sure there was great joy in Berkeley square, when the lost child was found again! The wicked uncle heard the news, and it made him so crazy, that he was placed in an insane hospital, where he died three years afterward. All Mary's wealth was restored to her; and her uncle Dallas loves her as if she were his own daughter. Thus the poor frightened little dove has at last found a sheltered home.

Betty Morris is married to a worthy young farmer. Their pretty cottage and well-stocked farm was a present from Mary Howard. Honest John has married Robert's youngest sister; and Mr. Dallas has given him five thousand pounds, and put him into good business.

Robert lost his New-Zealand wife two years after Mary's departure; and as he had no children, his heart yearned to return to England. He was fearful Mr. Dallas would not forgive him for the wickedness he had once purposed to do; but Mary urged him so much, that he at last came to London. She settled a handsome annuity on him, and he now lives very happily with his brother-in-law John. He says there is but one thing troubles him; and that is, he cannot go to London, because the boys run after him in such crowds, to see his tattooed face. As for Miss Howard, he says he "finds it hard work to treat her like a great lady, as she is; for notwithstanding her lace, and her diamonds, she will always seem to him like his own little darling Mary."

*   *   *   *   *   *   *   *   *

Duaterra was very angry when he first found Mary had gone to England : but a year or two after, he married one of his own tribe, and ceased to care about his mocking-bird. Every year Mary sends him hammers, and scissors, and nails, and beads, and such other things as she knows will please his savage fancy.

Little Mary is now an elegant young lady, accomplished in all that becomes a well-educated woman. I presume she has played most of the games mentioned in this little book. I am told she sews neatly, dances very gracefully, and handles her bow and arrow better than any woman in England. She is called a model of politeness ; for she has the same delicate consideration for the feeling of others, and the same love of making them happy, which made her so remarkably beloved when she was a little child.

As for the rude habits she naturally acquired in New-Zealand, she soon learned to change them. You would not believe she was ever among savages, unless you raised a cluster of curls and discovered Duaterra's tattooing.

THE PALACE OF BEAUTY.

A Fairy Tale.

In ancient times there lived two little princesses, one of whom was extremely beautiful, and the other dwarfish, dark-coloured, and deformed. One was named Rose, and the other Marion. The sisters did not live happily together. Marion hated Rose, because she was handsome, and every body praised her. She scowled, and her face absolutely grew black, when anybody asked her how her pretty little sister Rose did; and once she was so wicked as to cut off all her glossy, golden hair, and throw it in the fire. Poor Rose cried bitterly about it, but she did not scold, or strike her sister; for she was an amiable, gentle little being, as ever lived. No wonder all the family and all the neighbourhood disliked Marion—and no wonder her face grew uglier and uglier every day. The neighbours believed the infant Rose had been blessed by the fairies, to whom she owed her extraordinary beauty and exceeding goodness.

Not far from the Castle where the princesses resided, was a deep grotto, said to lead to the Palace of Beauty, where the Queen of the Fairies held her court. Some said Rose had fallen asleep there one day, when she had grown tired of chasing a butterfly, and that the Queen had dipped her in an immortal fountain, from which she had risen with the beauty of

an angel.* Marion often asked questions about this story;
but Rose always replied that she had been forbidden to speak
of it. When she saw any uncommonly brilliant bird, or but
terfly, she would sometimes exclaim, "Oh! how much that
looks like fairy-land!" But when asked what she knew about
fairy-land, she blushed, and would not answer.

Marion thought a great deal about this. "Why cannot I
go to the Palace of Beauty?" thought she; "and why may I
not bathe in the Immortal Fountain?"

One summer's noon, when all was still, save the faint twit-
tering of the birds, and the lazy hum of the insects, Marion
entered the deep grotto. She sat down on a bank of moss:
the air around her was as fragrant as if it came from a bed of
violets; and with a sound of far-off music dying on her ear,
she fell into a gentle slumber. When she awoke, it was evening; and she found herself in a small hall, where opal pillars
supported a rainbow roof, the bright reflection of which rested
on crystal walls, and a golden floor inlaid with pearls. All
around, between the opal pillars, stood the tiniest vases of
pure alabaster; in which grew a multitude of brilliant and fragrant flowers; some of them twining around the pillars, were
lost in the floating rainbow above. The whole of this scene
of beauty was lighted up by millions of fire-flies, glittering about

---

* There was a superstition, that whoever slept on fairy ground was carried away by
the fairies.

like wandering stars. While Marion was wondering at all this, a little figure of rare loveliness stood before her. Her robe was of green and gold; her flowing gossamer mantle was caught up on one shoulder with a pearl, and in her hair was a solitary star composed of five diamonds, each no bigger than a pin's point. And thus she sung;

The Fairy Queen
Hath rarely seen
Creature of earthly mould,
Within her door,
On pearly floor
Inlaid with shining gold.
Mortal, all thou seest is fair—
Quick thy purposes declare.

As she concluded, the song was taken up, and thrice repeated by a multitude of soft voices in the distance. It seemed as if birds and insects joined the chorus—the clear voice of the thrush was distinctly heard; the cricket kept time with his tiny cymbal; and ever and anon between the pauses, the sound of a distant cascade was heard, whose waters played a tune as they fell.

All these delightful sounds died away, and the Queen of the Fairies stood patiently awaiting Marion's answer. Courtesying low, and with a trembling voice, the little maiden said, " Will it please your majesty to make me as handsome as my sister Rose?" The Queen smiled: " I will grant your request,' said she, " if you will promise to fulfil all the conditions I im-

18

pose." Marion eagerly promised that she would. "The
Immortal Fountain," replied the queen, "is on the top of a
high, steep hill; at four different places fairies are stationed
around it, who guard it with their wands; none can pass them,
except those who obey my orders. Go home now; for one
week, speak no ungentle word to your sister—at the end of
that time, come again to the grotto."

Marion went home light of heart. Rose was in the garden
watering the flowers; and the first thing Marion observed, was
that her sister's sunny hair had suddenly grown as long and
beautiful as it had ever been. The sight made her angry; and
she was just about to snatch the water-pot from her hand with
an angry expression; but she remembered the fairy, and passed into the castle in silence. The end of the week arrived,
and Marion had faithfully kept her promise. Again she went
to the grotto. The Queen was feasting, when she entered the
hall. The bees brought honey-comb, and deposited it on the
small rose-coloured shells which adorned the crystal table;
gaudy butterflies floated about the head of the Queen, and
fanned her with their wings; the cucullo and the lantern-fly
stood at her side, to afford her light; a large diamond beetle
formed her splendid footstool; and when she had supped, a
dew-drop, on the petal of a violet, was brought for her royal
fingers.

When Marion entered, the diamond sparkles on the wings
of the fairies faded, as they always did in the presence of any-

thing not perfectly good; and in a few moments all the Queen's attendants vanished away, singing as they went,

The Fairy Queen
Hath rarely seen
Creature of earthly mould,
Within her door,
On pearly floor
Inlaid with shining gold.

"Mortal! hast thou fulfilled thy promise?" asked the Queen. "I have," replied the maiden. "Then follow me." Marion did as she was directed—and away they went, over beds of violets and mignionette. The birds warbled above their heads, and butterflies cooled the air, and the gurgling of many fountains came with a refreshing sound. Presently, they came to the hill, on the top of which was the Immortal Fountain. Its foot was surrounded by a band of fairies clothed in green gossamer, with their ivory wands crossed to bar the ascent. The Queen waved her wand over them, and immediately they stretched their thin wings and flew away. The hill was steep; and far, far up they went; and the air became more and more fragrant; and more and more distinctly they heard the sound of the waters falling in music. At length, they were stopped by a band of fairies clothed in blue, with their silver wands crossed. "Here," said the Queen, "our journey must end. You can go no farther until you have fulfilled the orders I shall give you. Go home now; for one month, do by your sister in all respects, as you would wish to have her do by you, were you Rose, and she Marion.". Marion promised, and departed. She found the task harder than the first had been. She could help speaking; but when Rose asked for any of her playthings, she found it difficult to give them gently and affectionately, instead of pushing them along; when Rose talked to her, she wanted to go away in silence; and when a pocket-mirror was found in her sister's room broken into a thousand pieces, she felt sorely tempted to conceal that she did the mischief. But she was so anxious to be made beautiful, that she did as she would be done by.

All the household remarked how Marion had changed. "I love her dearly," said Rose, "she is so good and amiable." "So do I," and "so do I," said a dozen voices. Marion blushed, and her eyes sparkled with pleasure. "How pleasant it is to be loved!" thought she.

At the end of the month, she went to the grotto. The fairies in blue lowered their silver wands, and flew away. They travelled on—the path grew steeper and steeper; but the fragrance of the atmosphere was redoubled; and more distinctly came the sound of the waters falling in music. Their course was stayed by a troop of fairies in rainbow robes and silver wands tipped with gold. In face and form, they were far more beautiful than any thing Marion had yet seen. "Here we must pause," said the Queen: "this boundary you cannot yet pass." "Why not?" asked the impatient Marion. "Because those must be very pure, who pass the rainbow fairies,"

replied the Queen. "Am I not very pure?" said Marion: "all the folks at the Castle tell me how good I have grown."

"Mortal eyes see only the outside," answered the Queen: "but those who pass the rainbow fairies must be pure in thought, as well as in action. Return home—for three months never indulge an envious or wicked thought. You shall then have a sight of the Immortal Fountain." Marion was sad at heart; for she knew how many envious thoughts and wrong wishes she had suffered to gain power over her.

At the end of the three months, she again visited the Palace of Beauty. The Queen did not smile when she saw her; but in silence led the way to the Immortal Fountain. The Green Fairies and the Blue Fairies flew away, as they approached; but the Rainbow Fairies bowed low to the Queen, and kept their gold-tipped wands firmly crossed. Marion saw that the silver specks on their wings grew dim; and she burst into tears. "I knew," said the Queen, "that you could not pass this boundary. Envy has been in your heart, and you have not driven it away. Your sister has been ill: and in your heart you wished that she might die, or rise from the bed of sickness deprived of her beauty. But be not discouraged; you have been several years indulging wrong feelings; and you must not wonder that it takes many months to drive them away."

Marion was very sad as she wended her way homeward. When Rose asked her what was the matter, she told her that she wanted to be very good, but she could not. "When I want to be good, I read my Bible, and pray," said Rose; "and I find God helps me to be good." Then Marion prayed that God would help her to be pure in thought; and when wicked feelings rose in her heart, she read her Bible, and they went away.

When she again visited the Palace of Beauty, the Queen smiled, and touched her playfully with her wand, then led the way to the Immortal Fountain. The silver specks on the wings of the Rainbow Fairies shone bright, as she approached them, and they lowered their wands, and sung as they flew away—

> Mortal, pass on,
> Till the goal is won,—
> For such, I ween,
> Is the will of our Queen.
> Pass on! pass on!

And now every footstep was on flowers, that yielded beneath their feet, as if their pathway had been upon a cloud. The delicious fragrance could almost be felt, yet it did not oppress the senses with its heaviness; and loud, clear, and liquid, came the sound of the waters as they fell in music. And now the cascade is seen leaping and sparkling over crystal rocks—a rainbow arch rests above it, like a perpetual halo: the spray falls in pearls, and forms fantastic foliage about the margin of the fountain. It has touched the webs woven among the grass, and they have become pearl-embroidered cloaks for the Fairy Queen. Deep and silent, below the foam, is the Immortal Fountain! Its amber-coloured waves flow over a golden bed; and as the fairies bathe in it, the diamonds in their hair glance like sun-beams on the waters.

"Oh! let me bathe in the fountain!" cried Marion, clasping her hands in delight. "Not yet," said the Queen. "Behold the Purple Fairies with golden wands that guard its brink!" Marion looked, and saw beings far lovelier than any her eye had ever rested on. "You cannot pass them yet," said the Queen. "Go home—for one year drive away all evil feelings, not for the sake of bathing in this fountain, but because goodness is lovely and desirable for its own sake Purify the inward motive, and your work is done."

This was the hardest task of all. For she had been willing to be good, not because it was right to be good, but because she wished to be beautiful. Three times she sought the grotto, and three times she left it in tears; for the golden specks grew dim at her approach, and the golden wands were still crossed, to shut her from the Immortal Fountain. The fourth time she prevailed. The Purple Fairies lowered their wands, singing,

Thou hast scaled the mountain,
Go, bathe in the fountain!
Rise fair to the sight
As an angel of light,—
Go, bathe in the fountain!

Marion was about to plunge in; but **the Queen** touched her, saying, " Look in the mirror of the waters.   Art thou not already as beautiful as heart can wish ?"

Marion looked at herself, and she saw that her eye sparkled with new lustre, that a bright colour shone through her cheeks, and dimples played sweetly about her mouth.   " I have not touched the Immortal Fountain," said she, turning in surprise to the Queen.   " True," replied the Queen ; " but its waters have been within your soul.   Know that a pure heart and a clean conscience are the only Immortal Fountain of Beauty."

When Marion returned, Rose clasped her to her bosom, and kissed her fervently.   " I know all," said she, " though I have not asked you a question.   I have been in fairy land, disguised as a bird, and I have watched all your steps.   When you first went to the grotto, I begged the Queen to grant your wish."

Ever after that, the sisters lived lovingly together.   It was the remark of every one, " How handsome Marion has grown ! The ugly scowl has departed from her face ; and the light of her eye is so mild and pleasant, and her mouth looks so smiling and good-natured, that, to my taste, I declare she is as handsome as Rose."

MAXIMS FOR HEALTH AND GRACEFULNESS.

EARLY rising, and the habit of washing frequently in pure cold water, are fine things for the health and complexion.

———

WALKING and other out-of-door exercises, cannot be too much recommended to young people. Even skating, driving hoop, and other boyish sports, may be practised to great advantage by little girls, provided they can be pursued within the inclosure of a garden, or court; in the street, they would of course be highly improper. It is true, such games are rather violent, and sometimes noisy; but they tend to form a vigorous constitution; and girls who are habitually lady-like, will never allow themselves to be rude and vulgar, even in play.

———

SHOES and garments for children should be quite large enough for ease, comfort, and freedom of motion.

———

CLEAN the teeth as much as twice a day, with a brush and pure water. The habit of always cleansing the teeth before retiring to rest, tends greatly to their preservation.

CHILDREN should eat simple food, and just as much of it as they need, and no more. Even the silly parrot will not eat merely to gratify her palate, when her appetite is satisfied.

Many a pimpled face and aching head is produced by eating too much.

A TENDENCY to stoop should be early corrected. It is very destructive to health. This habit, together with the very ungraceful one of running the chin out, may be cured by the practice of walking the room frequently with a heavy folio volume balanced on the head, without the aid of the hands. The Egyptian women, who go down to the Nile to bring up heavy burdens of water on their heads, are remarkable for erect forms and majestic motions.

LITTLE girls should be careful, whether walking or sitting, to turn their feet out. The habit of turning the feet toward each other is extremely awkward. The practice of shrugging the shoulders is still more so: they should always be carried as low as possible. These things are of very little consequence, compared with what relates to the mind and heart; but we cannot help acquiring habits; and it is better to acquire good than bad ones, even in the most trifling things.

THE beauty of the hair depends greatly upon keeping it perfectly clean and disentangled. Washing the hair with luke-warm soft water, with a little soap in it, and a thorough brushing afterward, is much better than the too frequent use of the ivory-comb; many, who take excellent care of their hair, do not use an ivory-comb at all. No women in the world are more distinguished for fine and glossy hair than the South-Sea islanders: it is said to be the effect of frequent bathing. Silk night-caps are more cool and healthy than cotton ones. The French comb children's hair entirely back from the forehead, after the fashion of our grandmothers. It is an excellent plan; for it checks its growing low upon the forehead and temples, and prevents the tendency to crossing the eyes so often produced by looking at the hair, when it falls in sight.

Physicians have agreed that it is better to keep the hair cut until the child is nine or ten years old. An abundance of hair at an early age, is apt to produce weak eyes, paleness, and head-ache; besides, the idea that hair is made coarse by frequent cutting in childhood, is entirely unfounded.

———

REGULAR hours for food, study, exercise, play, &c. have an excellent effect on the character, as well as the health.

MORAL MAXIMS.

THE most important of all earthly things, are purity of heart and correctness of principle. Intellect, wealth and beauty, are of little value compared with goodness; and unless these gifts are accompanied with goodness, they serve to make the possessor unhappy within herself, and disliked by her companions. Little children can have good principles, as well as grown people; the rules for forming them are few and simple.

1. Remember that God sees all your actions and all your thoughts. Be in the daily habit of prayer to him, and he will help you to cherish what is good, and drive away what is evil. I once saw a little girl kneel and pray, when she thought no one heard her, "Our Father, who art in heaven, forgive me for striking my little brother to-day; and help me not to strike him again; for oh! if he should die, how sorry I should be that I struck him." It was a simple and a holy prayer. God did help her to govern her quick temper; and when she was twelve years old, she was as mild and gentle as a lamb.

2. Never forget the Golden Rule, to do by others as you would have others do by you. Perhaps you have in your class a little girl, who has not been at school as much as yourself; and because she cannot get her lessons very readily, you laugh at her, and call her stupid. Were you in her place, should you like to be so treated? If your heart answers 'no.'

you may be sure your conduct has been wrong. Have you never spoken unamiably to a companion, merely because she took her station above you in the class? You can easily tell how well you should like such language, were you in her place.

Have you never made your older sisters a great deal of trouble, by your carelessness, disobedience, or obstinacy? Had you the care of a younger sister, should you not be grieved by such behaviour?

I will not mention any more instances in which this invaluable rule will serve as an unerring guide; there is no event in life, great or small, to which it may not be applied.

3. Deal frankly with all, particularly with your parents or guardian. Never attempt to conceal your actions, or your motives. If you have broken, or injured anything, go at once and avow it; and if you have been to blame in your intercourse with your companions, do not let silly pride, or false shame, prevent you from acknowledging it. You cannot conceal anything from God; and the attempt to deceive your friends will have a very bad influence on your heart.

4. When you have formed a good resolution, never put off the time for carrying it into execution. Every time a bad habit is indulged, it grows stronger and is more difficult to overcome.

5. Be as polite and amiable at home, as if you were among strangers. You need not learn the art from masters; the

observance of the Golden Rule will make you polite; for it will teach you to prefer the happiness and comfort of others to your own, even in the most trifling particulars. Above all, be polite, attentive, respectful, and affectionate to your parents. Good parents are the choicest blessings God ever gives. You can never do enough to repay them for their care of you.

6. Cherish love for your brothers and sisters. Let your words and actions be such toward them, as you wish they had been, should death separate you from each other.

7. Next to goodness, strive to obtain knowledge. Never forget, that by practice and perseverance *you can learn anything*.

8. Have a scrupulous regard to neatness of person. Broken strings and tangled hair, are signs that little girls are not very industrious or regular, in any of their habits.

A CUSTOM WORTHY IMITATION.

In Germany, the children all make it a rule to prepare Christmas presents for their parents, and brothers and sisters. Even the youngest contrive to offer something. For weeks before the important day arrives, they are as busy as little bees, contriving and making such things as they suppose will be most agreeable.

The great object is to keep each one ignorant of the present he or she is to receive, in order to surprise them when the offering is presented. A great deal of whispering, and innocent management, is resorted to, to effect this purpose; and their little minds are brimful of the happy business.

This is a most interesting and affectionate custom. I wish American little girls would exercise their ingenuity in making boxes, baskets, needle-books, &c. for the same purpose. Their hearts will be warmed with good feelings, while their fingers are acquiring skill; and they will find, as the Bible tells them, that " It is more blessed to give than to receive."

A distinguished English writer wrote the following simple
          Prayer for the use of his little Daughter.

Ere on my bed my limbs I lay,
God grant me grace my prayers to say!
O God! preserve my mother dear,
In health and strength for many a year;
And, oh! preserve my father, too,
And may I pay him reverence due;
And may I my best thoughts employ,
To be my parents' hope and joy.
Oh! likewise keep my brothers, both
From evil doings and from sloth;
And may we always love each other,
Our friends, our father, and our mother.
And still, O Lord! to me impart
An innocent and grateful heart,
That, after my last sleep, I may
Awake to thy eternal day!

APPLEWOOD BOOKS
Publishers of America's Living Past

OTHER APPLEWOOD TITLES YOU WILL ENJOY

❧

The Boy's Own Book
William Clarke

A Companion to *The Girl's Own Book*, with games,
tricks and amusements for every boy.
4 ½ x 5 ½, 320 pp., $12.95

The Education of a Daughter
Archbishop Fenelon

Written in 1687 by the Archbishop Fenelon of Gascony, and published
in 1847, *The Education of a Daughter* is filled with sound wisdom
on the ample subject of rearing both daughters and sons.
A constant reminder that good advice often gets better with age.
5 x 7 ¼, 160 pp., $9.95

The Mother's Book
Lydia Maria Child

Originally published in 1831, these instructions for mothers
on raising children are still applicable to today's parents.
5 x 8 ¼, 169 pp., $14.95

❧

Applewood Books, Box 27, Carlisle, MA 01741